chill

Other Simon Pulse nonfiction books you might enjoy

In Their Shoes:
Extraordinary Women Describe Their Amazing Careers
Deborah Reber

Doing It Right:
Making Smart, Safe, and Satisfying Choices About Sex
Bronwen Pardes

What If?:
Answers to Questions About What It Means
to Be Gay and Lesbian
Eric Marcus

From Simon Pulse/Beyond Words

Doable:
The Girls' Guide to Accomplishing Just About Anything
Deborah Reber

chill

Stress-Reducing Techniques for a
More Balanced, Peaceful You

DEBORAH REBER
ILLUSTRATED BY NERYL WALKER

Simon Pulse New York London Toronto Sydney New Delhi

A Note to the Reader

This book is intended to provide helpful and informative material on how you can relieve stress. You might find some of the techniques helpful, and others less so or not at all, but the hope is that by understanding what stress is and how others have learned to relieve it, you can minimize stress in your own life. The anecdotes and letters in the book are intended to be illustrative of experiences common to many teenagers rather than the actual experience of any particular person, and the names and identifying features of those providing anecdotes and letters have been changed. Please note that this book is sold with the understanding that the author and publisher are not engaged in rendering medical, health, or any other kind of personal professional services in the book. If you need or think you might need such services, please contact such a professional.

SIMON PULSE

An imprint of Simon & Schuster Children's Publishing Division

1230 Avenue of the Americas, New York, NY 10020

This Simon Pulse edition January 2015

Text copyright © 2008 by Deborah Reber

Interior illustrations copyright © 2008 by Neryl Walker

Cover illustration copyright © 2015 by Karina Granda

For information about special discounts for bulk purchases, please contact

Simon & Schuster Special Sales at 1-866-506-1949 or business@simonandschuster.com.

The Simon & Schuster Speakers Bureau can bring authors to your live event.

For more information or to book an event contact the Simon & Schuster Speakers Bureau

at 1-866-248-3049 or visit our website at www.simonspeakers.com.

The text of this book was set in Avenir LT Std.

Cover designed by Karina Granda

Interior designed by Mike Rosamilia, based on the original interior

by Joel Avirom and Jason Snyder

Manufactured in the United States of America

10 9 8 7 6 5 4 3 2 1

Library of Congress Control Number 2007936784

ISBN 978-1-4814-2810-1 (hc)

ISBN 978-1-4814-2809-5 (pbk)

ISBN 978-1-4814-4045-5 (eBook)

To my sister, Shelly

ACKNOWLEDGMENTS

For their support, guidance, and ability to help me de-stress while writing *Chill*, I am filled with gratitude toward:

My husband, Derin: Thank you for your seemingly endless support, your keen observations, and, most of all, your love.

My son, Asher: For your impromptu hugs, infectious laughter, and constant reminder of how to live in the moment.

My mom and dad, Dale and MaryLou: For always listening to my babbling commentary about the progress of this book.

My sister, Michele: Thanks for being the ace in my back pocket and making yourself continually available to read and comment on draft after draft (after draft).

My in-laws, Barbara and David: For your encouragement and interest in my writing ventures.

My "support team" of Alice, AnneMarie, Ed, and Renée: Thank you for always being there for me!

My dog, Baxter: For being the perfect excuse to take running breaks while on tight deadlines.

My "girls' night girls"—Alison, Mardi, Sara, Gina, and Elizabeth: Thanks for reminding me of the importance of downtime when feeling the crunch.

Lisa Viscardi: For your friendship and for sharing your insights on organization with the readers.

Renée Adams: For your thoughtful review and contribution of material on zoning out and tuning in.

My agent, Susan Schulman: Thank you for being such a pro and for being so continually supportive of my mission.

My editors, Anica Mrose Rissi and Patrick Price: Thank you for your professionalism, for your enthusiasm, and for making this book so much better through your thoughtful comments and contributions.

Michelle Nagler: Thank you for bringing this idea to me and being such a wonderful advocate.

Bethany Buck: Thank you for championing this book and giving me the opportunity to update it for the next generation of teen girls.

Neryl Walker: Thank you for bringing such beauty and sophistication to the pages of this book through your illustrations.

The incredible designers who brought the content of this book to life—Russell Gordon, Joel Avirom, Jason Snyder, and Meghan Day Healey: You are so good at what you do!

To my power team at Simon & Schuster, who put their all into making this book a success: Bethany Buck, Paul Crichton, Katherine Devendorf, Jaime Feldman, Lucille Rettino, Bess Braswell, Kelly Stocks, Carey O'Brien, Victor Iannone, Jim Conlin, and Beth Sue Rose.

And last but not least, to the girls behind the anecdotes throughout *Chill*: Thank you for sharing your stories with me. . . . This book is for you!

CONTENTS

LOOKING OUT

LOOKING IN

GETTING PHYSICAL

INTRODUCTION

Life can be stressful. You're balancing schoolwork, sports, extracurriculars, dating, an after-school job, your social media feeds, and trying to figure out what comes next—plus juggling all the demands your parents, teachers, and friendships place on you, not to mention the expectations you put on *yourself*.

Trust me . . . *I know*. Like you, my daily life is filled with stress, but over the years, I've come up with all kinds of techniques to deal. Of course, every now and then I still teeter on the brink of a full-fledged, stress-induced meltdown, but I can usually find the right strategy to get me through the crisis. Just last week, however, I was put to the test. Here's a play-by-play:

I'm in New York City—102nd Street and First Avenue, to be exact. I'm sitting in the back of a taxi on my way to JFK airport. It's been an awesome week, but I'm ready to get back home to Seattle, where my husband, son, and dog are awaiting my arrival. I'm looking forward to a calm, relaxing flight where I can zone out with my iPod and enjoy a few last hours of uninterrupted work time and a bag or two of salted peanuts.

This is the clear image I have in my head when the traffic on First Avenue screeches to a halt. The taxi begins to crawl, a half mile an hour . . . *tops*. Traveling the distance of two city blocks, which should have taken thirty seconds, stretches into fifteen minutes.

We finally inch our way over the Triborough Bridge and into Queens, but the traffic there is no better. Though I had left my friend's apartment in plenty of time to drive to the airport, my spirits plummet as I catch sight of the sea of brake lights ahead of me.

It's 5:28 p.m. My flight leaves at six thirty and I'm still a good ten miles out.

Anxiety pours through my veins. My heart races. I begin imagining the worst-case scenarios—shelling out a couple hundred bucks to get on another flight or holing up in a fleabag motel off Route 495 so I can fly out first thing in the morning.

Then a voice in my head chimes in to stop my pending panic.

Hold on a sec, Deb. You can handle this without freaking out. Center yourself. Take some deep breaths.

I do.

The minutes pass.

5:45 p.m. The centering stops working. Time for another technique.

Visualize, I say to myself. *Visualize the traffic opening up. Picture yourself sitting comfortably on your flight an hour from now.*

I do.

The minutes pass.

5:56 p.m. I'm still anxious and even more convinced I'll be missing my flight.

Come on, Debbie. You're writing a book on how to de-stress. You've got to find a way to cope, I say to myself.

So I dig down deep inside my core and make one last attempt to manage my angst, which by this time is causing beads of sweat bigger than a Seattle raindrop to drip off my forehead. I decide to change my thinking in order to change the way I'm feeling, and I tell myself the following:

Stressing out won't make it any more likely that I'll make my flight. So I can either freak out about it, or I can lean back and relax . . . either way, the outcome will be the same. And frankly, relaxing sounds a lot better than having a breakdown in the backseat of a cab.

So I make the choice to chill out.

And it works.

EPILOGUE: I pulled up to JFK at 6:04 p.m., officially missing the cutoff time to check in for my flight. Luckily, the Delta folks hooked me up, escorted me through security (where, because I hadn't had a chance to put my liquids in a Ziploc, I had to kiss about eighty dollars' worth of product good-bye, but *whatever*), and ran with me to make sure I got aboard my flight. It wasn't pretty, but I made it. I collapsed into my nonreclining seat in the last row, sweaty and sucking wind from the dash. I'd made it just in the nick of time . . . the nick of time to sit on the tarmac for two hours because of an airplane "traffic" jam. But hey, I'm not complaining.

Whether you're racing to catch a flight, balancing a ridiculously overbooked schedule, or navigating a complicated situation among your circle of friends, stress is a universal experience (unless, perhaps, you're a Buddhist monk . . . I don't think they're allowed to be stressed). Sometimes stress catches you off guard—the result of a crisis, an emergency, or some unexpected turn of events. Other times stress simply builds up over time—the unfortunate result of month after month of being overscheduled, overachieving . . . overwhelmed. Sometimes stress comes as a side-effect of simply getting through day-to-day life, full of worries over things like safety, college dreams, and the unknowns of the future.

Regardless of the specific cause, stress always harms you most when you're off balance—when one or more aspects of your being (body, mind, and soul) is not getting the attention it deserves. When you're off balance, you're not able to handle the ups and downs of life as well as you could, because you don't feel centered and are easily thrown off track. The slightest bump in the road can turn your world upside down. Unfortunately, this is the way most of us live, most of the time.

You might be thinking: *How can I make room for balance in my life when there's so much pressure to "do" and "be" everything?*

That's where this book comes in. The most important step in finding balance is to have periodic personal "check-ins"—connecting with yourself and how you're doing on a physical, emotional, and spiritual level. Sometimes you might not even realize how much stress you've been building up until it reaches the point where you're completely overwhelmed. You can avoid a total meltdown by paying attention to the minor stresses in your life and taking note of the times you feel out of sorts or off balance. When you start feeling as though things are spiraling out of your control, making even one small adjustment to your schedule or taking a short "time-out" for yourself can put things back into balance.

This book presents all kinds of approaches for stomping out the stresses in your life. Within each chapter, you'll find dozens of practical tips that you can try out in your life right now. You may find that one of these techniques works for you no matter what kind of challenge you're up against.

Or you may need to use different techniques to tackle different stress-inducing factors. Experiment and adjust your approach until you find the right match—inside these pages is a method that will work for you.

But wait . . . there's more! Inside *Chill* you'll find anecdotes and tips from successful women and other teens, quizzes to help you get connected to yourself and find your own best de-stressing style, and suggestions for incorporating stress-relieving strategies into your life seamlessly and without too much effort. Lastly, at the end of each chapter are ideas for things to explore on your own in your journal (if you don't already keep one, jump ahead to Chapter 9 for tips on how to get started), as well as suggested "affirmations" that can help you remember the power you already have within to conquer your stress.

Before you get started, I must warn you: Some of my stress-relief suggestions might seem to be adding *more* to your "to do" list. But sometimes taking even ten minutes to do something positive to reduce your stress (like going for a walk or meditating or organizing your work space) will actually give you back hours of a less-stressed life in the long run.

Believe it or not, you already have the ability and the power to handle any stressors that life throws your way. All you need is to know how to do it. Read *Chill* with an open mind and see which techniques resonate. You don't have to be stressed if you don't want to, so make the choice to say no to stress in your life.

To get the most out of *Chill*, dive into some bonus content, and get on the fast track to applying these strategies and ideas to your own life, download your free *Chill* workbook at www.debbiereber.com.

Here's to a more balanced, peaceful you!

1
WHAT *IS* STRESS?

Stress seems to be on just about everyone's minds these days. I get tons of e-mails and letters from teen girls sharing their personal tales of stress and angst in their lives. So how do *you* define stress?

> *Stress is the feeling you get when you're taking on too much, or people are demanding on you too much.*
>
> **—ZOE, AGE 17**

> *I would define stress as being overwhelmed with a certain problem or person.* **—ALIA, AGE 16**

> *Stress is tension, whether emotional or physical. You can be stressed out about friendship troubles, or you can be stressed out about lack of sleep. You can get impatient in a long line at the grocery store, or your body can be stressed out by overexerting yourself in an exercise or sport.*
>
> **—GWYN, AGE 15**

All great definitions. Here's how the American Academy of Pediatrics defines stress: "[Stress is] the uncomfortable feeling you get when you're worried, scared, frustrated, or overwhelmed. It is caused by emotions, but it affects your mood and your body."

That definition might be straightforward enough, but stress sure doesn't feel straightforward to deal with. Yes, it's a normal part of life, but that doesn't mean it won't take a toll. Let stress run rampant and your mind, body, and soul will pay the price.

The Origins of Stress

Have you ever been in a situation where you went from calm to terrified in a split second? Maybe you were jolted awake in the middle of the night by a suspicious noise coming from inside your house. Or maybe you stepped into a busy intersection just as a car darted out of nowhere and narrowly missed hitting you. Maybe you were water-skiing, and, as you waited for the boat to swing around and pick you up, your mind turned to the movie *Jaws*, and you nearly freaked out big-time.

When you're thrust into a situation that feels dangerous, scary, or potentially life-threatening, your body switches to autopilot, and your nervous system takes over. Once your brain makes an internal announcement that something is wrong, your body responds by automatically releasing the hormone adrenaline into the blood stream. That's when the party really gets started. The adrenaline affects you by:

- increasing your heart rate (so you can take in more oxygen in case you need to run or exert yourself)

- raising your blood pressure (a result of your heart beating faster and your blood vessels constricting)

- sending more blood to your muscles so you'll be ready to react quickly and with power

Your body also releases cortisol, another hormone that works with adrenaline to:

- give you a quick burst of energy

- improve your memory

- increase your ability to withstand pain

If you've ever experienced a surge of adrenaline, or an "adrenaline rush," you might have noticed that things suddenly appeared to be happening in slow motion. Maybe you felt a rush of blood to your arms, legs, hands, or feet. Or maybe you broke out in a sweat, or suddenly felt shaky and nauseous. These are all classic symptoms of the "fight-or-flight response," a subconscious preparation by your body to do what it takes— stay and fight or turn and run—to survive any situation. They are also the classic symptoms of what we call stress.

In emergencies, stress can be a *good* thing. It's a survival tool, and a pretty efficient one at that. Stress isn't always a negative in your day-to-day life, either. It's stress that gives you that extra *oomph* while you're playing in the state soccer tournament, or when you're pushing to meet an impossible deadline. Small amounts of stress can keep you on your toes and push you to perform at your highest level. But what happens when you're dealt too much?

When Stress Doesn't Go Away

Just as your body's stress responses switch on during an emergency, they're supposed to switch off once the crisis has passed. Your heart rate should go back to normal, the sweating should stop, and the queasy feeling in your stomach should vanish.

But the problem comes in when your body repeatedly gets tricked into responding to stresses that aren't life threatening. Anxiety about next week's midterm can trigger the same fight-or-flight response as a serious threat. But since you don't actually need your survival hormones to get through your midterm, you're left with extra adrenaline and cortisol hanging around. The result? Chronic stress. Your body starts exhibiting classic stress symptoms *all the time*. Instead of giving you a boost to power through an emergency, the stress starts wearing you down. And that's when the trouble begins.

What Stress Does

Being seriously stressed out can cause all kinds of not-so-pleasant side effects, including:

- trouble sleeping

- tense muscles and muscle pain

- stomachaches, digestion problems, and/or constipation

- headaches, including migraines

- irritability and moodiness

- feeling down about everything

- impaired cognitive functioning

- unexpected emotional outbursts (such as crying or laughing for no reason)

- an irregular heartbeat or rapid heart rate

- lowered immunity (being more susceptible to illness or rashes)

- difficulty concentrating

- acne

Dealing with even one of these symptoms on a regular basis would wreak havoc on your peace factor. And when your stress runs rampant, it's also potentially damaging to your long-term health. Overstressed teens are at a much higher risk for developing depression, panic or anxiety disorders, and drug abuse problems as adults.

The Stress Roller Coaster

Once you buckle up for a ride on the stress roller coaster, it can sometimes be hard to climb off. Here's an example of how stress feeds on itself in a vicious cycle:

You feel anxious about something → you lose sleep → you're constantly tired → you rely on sugar and caffeine to perk you up → you become nutritionally imbalanced → you lack the energy to do anything about what you originally felt anxious about → you feel more anxiety and stress (and back to the beginning again)

You've probably already come up with some healthy ways to release your stress, but sometimes you might be coping in unhealthy ways too—getting into fights or lashing out at parents and friends, keeping your emotions and anxieties bottled up inside, bullying other people, or experimenting with drinking, doing drugs, engaging in risky sexual behavior, or cutting.

You can't always control the stressful situations that life throws your way, but you *can* control how you deal with your stress. To find your best stress solution, you need to figure out what it is you're so stressed out about in the first place. Read on to find out what teens everywhere say are their biggest stress sources. Chances are, you'll realize you're not alone.

WHAT'S YOUR SECRET FOR STOMPING OUT STRESS?

I write a lot of poetry and songs to relieve my stress . . . it helps to get everything out.   —DEVIN, AGE 15

My technique for relieving stress is running on the treadmill and listening to my favorite music. Also, just reading a book or magazine while listening to music is stress-relieving for me.
                                    —SAMANTHA, AGE 16

I've kept diaries since I was eight years old, and I write almost every night. It relaxes me and helps me fall asleep.
                                          —ABIGAIL, AGE 18

I make sure I have alone time.   —ALYSSA, AGE 16

TIME-OUT:
FACING THE FUTURE

During the writing of this book, the US was slowly crawling its way out of a recession. The job market, especially for entry-level positions, is particularly tight, even with a four-year college degree, and students are drowning in loan debt that makes it more and more difficult for them to have a decent standard of living as young, independent adults.

There's no way to predict what will happen with the job market and economy in years to come, but the not knowing can be just as stressful, especially for teens looking ahead to what's next.

The truth is, it can be hard to dream big when everywhere you turn there's a reminder about just how hard things can be. It's enough to make even the most self-possessed, optimistic girl have a bit of a meltdown.

LET IT GO

There are many strategies to help you deal with future stress freak-outs, but the most powerful one is to **let go of what you can't control**. Remind yourself that what happens in the future is no more in your control than whether or not it's going to rain Sunday or which numbers will be drawn in the next Mega Millions lottery.

By holding on to worry and stress over the "what ifs" (*What if I can't find a job? What if my career dreams don't pan out? What if the economy tanks again and I have to live at home until I'm thirty?*), you're essentially trying to control the future, as if your anxiety is actually a super power you can use to *will* the future to align with what you want.

Um, that doesn't work.

In fact, as I write in chapter eight, dwelling on fear and negativity can actually bring more fear and negativity into your life. And that's pretty much the opposite of what we're going for when it comes to reducing stress.

So, *let it go*.

And yes, I'm aware this is one of those easier-said-than-done kind of situations. So here are some more tips to make letting it go easier and, as a result, bring you more peace about what's to come:

Stay in the here and now. Since the past has already happened and can't be changed, and the future is a great big unknown, the best bet to experiencing more peace in your life is to *stay in the present*. How you choose to feel and what you choose to do in this moment is really the only thing completely within your control. To stay in the here and now, really be "in it," whatever "it" is. If you're baking cookies, enjoy all the smells and tastes and textures that go along with that. If you're dodging puddles in a cross-country meet, think about how your body feels as it glides down the path. When you find yourself spinning off into future unknowns, snap yourself back to the present.

Go back to gratitude. As I write in chapter seven, gratitude is a great way to bring attention to what is working in your life instead of focusing on what isn't or dwelling on unknowns that might feel big and scary. The simple act of taking five minutes to appreciate even little things you are grateful for can result in an instant mind shift.

Get inspired by others. Read the memoirs and biographies of people who've overcome challenges in their lives and gone on to accomplish incredible things. Not only will this help you reset your perspective, but it will give you a burst of inspiration and the reminder that you can do anything you set your mind to.

Be curious. Turning your worry into curiosity will transform the energy surrounding your thoughts about the future. Curiosity is about things like possibility, unlimited options, and what could be. And unlike the heavy anxiousness of worry, curiosity is light and exciting and hopeful. So instead of thinking thoughts like, *I'm worried I won't reach my future dreams,* think *I'm so curious to see where my passions and interests take me!*

And lastly . . .

Remember that you are creative, resourceful, and whole. It's true. You have what it takes to create whatever you want to create with your life. Trust in yourself and in your ability to make smart choices and figure it out as you go along.

2
WHAT'S EATING YOU?

One thing's for certain—life is complicated. And the things that stress us out are no exception. Here's fifteen-year-old Simone's story:

I met my first best friend when I was little, but only in the past few years have things gotten out of control. At first it was just stupid little things, like she would find another friend and ditch me until she got bored of her. Then she'd come back to me and act like nothing had happened. She did this repeatedly, and it really lowered my self-esteem. This went on for at least a few years, until we got into high school. That's when it got worse. Of course, she found a new friend again and she completely ignored me. She shut me out and pretended like I wasn't in her life at all. I wasn't going to have any of it, so I tried to work it out between the three of us: me, her, and her new "best friend." Then the new friend did everything she could to prevent me from keeping my friendship—spreading nasty rumors, getting other people to gang up on me . . . it got really bad.

Sound familiar? With social pressures like this, no wonder friendships are a major source of any teen's daily dose of stress. And that's just the tip of the iceberg.

Here are the top contenders for the prestigious title of "Things Most Likely to Create Stress and Angst in Your Life":

- Self-Identity

- College and Career Dreams

- Friendships

- Romantic Relationships

- School Realities

- Family Life

- Global Issues

- Yourself

SELF-IDENTITY

I'm always feeling stress about making sure I look good and maintaining the image that people expect of me.
—HAYLIE, AGE 16

Who am I? That's the million-dollar question. If you're like most teens, you spend a lot of time trying to figure out who you are, what you like, what you stand for, what your sexual orientation is, what you want to look like, how and where you fit in, and what kind of person you want to be.

This stressor is especially difficult to deal with because the media culture—TV shows, websites, magazines, advertisements, *everything*—bombards you with the message that you're not okay the way you are. Unless you live on a deserted island, your self-confidence is constantly being challenged to meet an impossible standard of perfection.

Coming to terms with the changes going on in your body, feeling overwhelming uncertainty about the way you look, or having negative or unhealthy thoughts about your appearance, all while you're also trying to figure out who you are *aside* from your looks, can cause major stress. As thirteen-year-old Cecelia says so aptly, "I get stressed over things like clothes not fitting at American Eagle because I'm too big for them." Unfortunately, there is no one-size-fits-all policy for teenhood.

Do you have stresses related to your self-identity?
Write them down here:

_____

_____

_____

_____

_____

_____

_____

_____

_____

_____

_____

I go to an all-girls school where all the girls are obsessed with getting good grades so they can get into Harvard or Yale and then get a high-paying job as a doctor or something like that. I'm constantly being told, "Do this to get into college!" or "Oh, you shouldn't do that . . . that looks bad on a résumé." Seriously, how much does one bad high school grade or silly extracurricular play into the span of your whole life? I thought this was supposed to be the best time of life, and I just don't understand why people turn it into an audition for college.

—HANNAH, AGE 16

Hannah makes a good point. Big dreams can come at a high price if you don't find a way to keep things in perspective. Pressure over grades, course loads, SAT scores, extracurricular activities, and class rank—it's enough to push even the most grounded girl over the edge.

I wish I could say that academic stress is much ado about nothing, but unfortunately, it's based on a pressure-filled reality. The number of students applying to college each year has hit record highs, and it's expected to keep rising. Couple that with the fact that many colleges are actually enrolling fewer students each year, and it's easy to understand why competition to get into most schools is becoming incredibly fierce.

And though the US is in recovery from a recent recession, the economy and the job market haven't fully bounced back. Students know that their best chance of landing a coveted post-college gig is to do whatever it takes to stand out.

You may be up for the challenge, but you're also probably paying the price of this academic rat race by:

- juggling a jam-packed schedule filled with sports, clubs, and other extracurricular activities and little or no time for chilling out

- obsessing over your GPA, your SAT and ACT scores, and class rank

- feeling immense pressure to load up on honors and AP classes or community college courses in high school

- experiencing competition among friends over college admittance (who gets in where, who gets accepted early admission, who gets wait-listed)

- having extremely high expectations placed on you (by your teachers and coaches, your parents, and yourself)

- feeling the need to do something exceptional outside of school, like create a nonprofit or get accepted to present at a TED youth conference or launch a successful YouTube channel

Talk about stress! Ask a twenty- or thirty-year-old what she wants to do with the rest of her life, and there's a good chance she won't even have a clue. Why should *you* be expected to have it all figured out?

What do you stress about when it comes to your future (college, career, etc.)? Write about it here:

_____
_____
_____

My group of friends, five of us in total, decided we were all going to prom together with our dates. We were all set with a table for ten. Well, as it turns out, one of our friends changed her mind and decided she and her date were going to go with his friends. Then two more of my friends decided they didn't want to bring dates. Since we couldn't fill a table anymore, the organizers decided to split us all up, and now most of us are sitting at tables with people we don't even get along with. Nothing is going as planned, everyone is turning on each other, and we're all stressed out like crazy. **—CHLOE, AGE 18**

Perhaps some of the most complicated stressors that crop up in your day-to-day existence are related to your social life. Because the dynamics within your social circle are unique, there's no one simple solution for every friendship dilemma. Friendships are so intense that when problems arise they can be all-consuming—affecting your sleep, your ability to concentrate, and your overall peace of mind.

Lump that in with the peer pressures you're facing, and you have a full menu of possible social stressors to deal with at any given time. Here are just a few you may be all too familiar with:

- having difficulty making friends or finding a BFF

- feeling pressure to be popular or fit in at school

- trying to be seen as a nonconformist

- feeling left out or being ostracized by a clique

- wanting to be perceived as cool

- feeling pressure to dress a certain way

- feeling pressure to experiment with drinking, drugs, and sex

- being labeled by your peers

- managing and protecting your online reputation

What are your social stresses? Write about them here:

_____

_____

_____

_____

_____

_____

_____

ROMANTIC RELATIONSHIPS

My boyfriend is a great guy, but lately he's been partying at least once or twice a week and getting high. He says that he hasn't been happy lately because of some problems he's been having with his friends. I asked him if I made him happy and he said that I do, but that we hardly see each other and that stresses him out more, which makes him want to get high. I also worry about his partying because he has health problems, but when I try to talk with him about it, he tells me it's not a big deal and that I shouldn't worry. **—LYNDSEY, AGE 16**

Your friendships may be complicated, but chances are they're on par with the high-stakes drama and angst that go along with many romantic relationships. *Does he really like me? Should we have sex? Is he cheating on me? Will we still be together after graduation?* If you're in a same-sex relationship, you may be dealing with the stress of intolerance and lack of understanding among some of your peers or your family. And even if you're not in a relationship, that doesn't mean you're off the hook—there's pressure to find the perfect significant other, snag a date for the spring dance, get positive attention from your crush.

Lastly, there's the stress surrounding the very real and very serious potential consequences of risky sexual behavior, such as pregnancy and STDs. It's enough to make you want to crawl into a hole and hold off on dating until you're twenty-five (but then, who would you go to prom with?).

What are your stresses when it comes to love, sex, and relationships? Write about them here:

_____

_____

_____

_____

_____

_____

_____

_____

_____

> *Just last year, there was this guy who was always talking*
> *about getting everyone back (for doing nothing, too . . . we*
> *left him alone with his friends and he seemed completely*
> *fine). Then he set a fire and threatened to bring a gun to*
> *school and kill everyone in his class. I hate having to worry*
> *about that stuff in order to get a good education.*
>
> **—JORDAN, AGE 12**

Academic pressure isn't the only stressful thing happening at school. No school is immune from incidents of physical, emotional, and cyberbullying and harassment. All it takes is negative attention from one person to turn your days upside down.

Then there's the darkest side of school life—students bringing weapons to school and on-campus violence. Sadly, school shootings are on the rise, and though the chances of your school being directly impacted by violence are slim, that doesn't mean you won't stress about the possibility, especially when tragedies at other schools seem to regularly make the news. More than half the teens polled for an article in *Teen Vogue* said they believe a murderous rampage could erupt at their school.

Do you have anxiety about bullying or violence at school?
Write about it here:

_____

_____

_____

_____

_____

_____

One of my biggest stressors is all of the fighting that goes on in my family.   **—SOPHIE, AGE 16**

I spend a lot of time worrying about the health of my grandparents.   **—NICOLE, AGE 18**

Whether your family resembles the Cleavers, the Simpsons, or the Brady Bunch, no home life is perfect. Stressors lurk everywhere. To start with, there's the pressure that comes from parents and relatives about the grades you should get, the extracurricular activities you should excel in, the way you should dress, the friends you should have, the chores you should do, the kind of person you should be.

Even if your parents are super supportive of your goals and choices, they can still add to your stress. *Are your parents stressed out?* Then you're at higher risk of becoming stressed. *Are your folks overly concerned about their own professional and financial success?* If so, chances are you'll grow up worrying about the same things. *Do your parents stress about their looks?* Then you might have been trained to do the same. No wonder stressing out can be a hard habit to break.

Lastly, there are the stressors that come from challenges that arise within the family unit, any one of which could turn your world upside down in a heartbeat, such as:

- having your parents divorce or remarry

- being shuttled back and forth between homes

- having a parent lose their job and seeing your family tossed into financial uncertainty

- facing the sickness or death of a family member

- having a sibling go through a crisis

- having a parent in trouble with the law

- living in a home where there is physical and/or emotional abuse

- having a lousy relationship with your parents

- witnessing family members fight

- having to move to another town, state, or country

What stresses do you experience in your family life?
Write about them here:

_____

_____

_____

_____

_____

GLOBAL ISSUES

I'm stressed about the destroying and removing of our rain forests. There could be so many cures for sicknesses from the plants, and they also give us a huge amount of oxygen. **—MADDY, AGE 13**

I hear all kinds of stuff about global warming, like how New York may be underwater if oceans rise too much and how those poor polar bears are losing all their ice. It really makes me scared. **—HOPE, AGE 12**

Climate change, genocide, war, famine, natural disasters, health epidemics, violence in your neighborhood or community—there's no shortage of global and local issues to put your body and mind into stress overdrive.

Concern about the world's problems can be a positive thing—it can inspire and motivate people to work toward solutions. But when a concern turns into obsessive worry or continual angst, you can build up internal stress that has no way to escape.

What are your stresses about what's going on in the world?

_____

_____

_____

_____

_____

_____

_____

_____

YOURSELF

I put a lot of pressure on myself about my grades. They always have to be perfect, so I'll spend hours studying and freaking out because I can't remember the information, and then because I stayed up half the night studying I'm tired when I roll out of bed at six thirty a.m., so I don't end up looking my best. Then I spend all day stressing about how bad I look. It's an endless cycle! **—BELLA, AGE 13**

Do you ever judge yourself harshly when you look in the mirror? Ever beat yourself up over a grade on a test? Ever think you should be achieving more or being the best at everything you try? At the end of the day, no matter how much pressure you feel from outside factors, there's no doubt the biggest source of your stress is you. The pressure you place on yourself far outweighs what anything or anyone else can dish out. Luckily, this source of stress is in your control. (I'll show you how to get a grip on it later in the book.)

What pressures and expectations do you put on yourself?

_____
_____
_____
_____
_____
_____
_____
_____

Now that you've identified some of your major stressors, let's get to the good stuff! Read on and learn how to start reducing your stress *today*.

TAKING
ACTION

3

TIME MANAGEMENT

Do you ever feel like you should be featured in the *Guinness World Records* book for the number of responsibilities you juggle at once? The way I see it, there are only a few options: Hire a personal assistant (or three), clone yourself so you can be in two places at once, or become skilled in the art of time management. Since the first two options are probably beyond your means, time management it is.

In the simplest terms, time management is about getting real. It's about figuring out how long certain tasks will take you and making a plan for getting them all done. It might not sound glamorous, but time management is one of the most powerful tools you can wield when it comes to creating a more stress-free existence. If you can master this concept, you'll knock out so much stress you might not even need to read the rest of this book! (Just kidding . . . keep reading!)

TIME MANAGEMENT: Organizing your schedule, making the best use of your limited time, and creating a realistic plan for accomplishing everything on your "to do" list. Ideal for reducing stress related to:

- having a maxed-out schedule full of school and extracurricular activities

- juggling multiple assignments due in the same period of time

- facing pressure regarding schoolwork or college application deadlines

- feeling constantly overwhelmed and anxious

There's no one right way to manage your time. Sometimes good time management means creating a plan for accomplishing specific tasks each day, week, or month. Other times, it's about being honest with yourself about what you can and can't accomplish. Sometimes it's about arranging your schedule to fit in an extra task or event that's important to you. Sometimes it's about assessing all you've got going on in your life and realizing when you need to take something off your plate (see Chapter 5 for more on saying no to an opportunity or obligation).

One thing time management always involves? *Figuring out the tasks at hand and coming up with a plan for executing them.* Stress often stems from a fear of the unknown or being just plain overwhelmed about everything that's going on (*I've never juggled three honors classes before* or *Are there enough hours in the weekend to finish my assignment and spend time with my family, my best friend, and my boyfriend?*). Time management techniques take the mystery out of the equation. Plainly put: *PLAN OF ACTION = PEACE OF MIND.*

WHAT TO DO

My book *Doable: The Girls' Guide to Accomplishing Just About Anything* is all about how to achieve your goals and get it all done, but here is the CliffsNotes version as it relates to time management. How you go about managing your time will depend on the task(s) or event(s) you're dealing with. Creating a schedule for a school project will be different from figuring out how to juggle your busy social life.

No matter the goal, the first step is always the same: *getting real*. To do that, you've got to be honest about three things:

1. what it is you have to do (everything that's on your plate)

2. how long each task will take (your best guesstimate is fine)

3. how you'll make the time to get it all done

When you're up against the clock, don't freak out—make a plan. You can tackle any project or assignment by:

1. creating a detailed list of the tasks involved. Include every last step that goes into completing your project or assignment.

2. figuring out how long each task will take. Your best guesstimate is fine.

3. marking the final deadline on a calendar

4. backtracking from the deadline and creating mini-goals for when to complete each task from step one

5. adding tasks to your daily "to do" list, so you can work toward your bigger goal a little bit every day

WHAT YOU'LL NEED

All you really need to become a time management guru is a place to keep track of your tasks and write up a plan, as well as a calendar so you can look at your time in terms of hours, days, weeks, and months. Here are some ideas:

- **White board:** For creating a regular weekly or daily schedule, a large erasable white board that you can mark up and put somewhere obvious (like on your bedroom wall or the back of your door) works great. If you want to go all out, you can even buy wallpaper made of erasable whiteboard material, or paint your wall with chalkboard paint.

- **Day planner:** They may seem prehistoric, but good old-fashioned day planners (a yearly calendar with room for making notes each day) are invaluable tools for marking deadlines and keeping track of dates, sporting events, concerts, sleepovers, and other activities.

- **Notebook:** Don't want to fork over the money for a day planner? A simple spiral-bound notebook will work just fine. Create headings for whatever task you're scheduling, and fill the pages with your timelines, charts, and daily or weekly "to do" lists.

- **Online calendar:** Most computers come with a built-in calendar that allows you to color-code events and create alarms for deadlines, as well as view your calendar by day, week, or month. Or, try a cloud program like Google Calendar so you can access your ToDos everywhere.

- **Smart Phones or Tablets:** What could be better (or easier) than keeping your schedule, calendar, and to-do lists on your smart phone or tablet? Use the apps that come standard with your device or download one of the many free or cheap apps specifically designed to help you schedule your life.

Mapping Out Your Work

To help you get started, check out these example project templates. If you want to edit and print them out for yourself, you can download them from my website, www.debbiereber.com.

A TERM PAPER OR LONG-TERM CLASS PROJECT

[NAME OF PROJECT HERE]   Due Date:

Task List	Length of Time to Complete	Deadline
Brainstorming		
Library research		
Online research		
Group or team meetings		
Develop outline		
Organize notes		
Write bibliography		
Write first draft		
Edit first draft		
Complete revised draft		
Insert graphics/images		
Proofread and review		
Format and print out		

A CLASS WITH FREQUENT QUIZZES, TESTS, OR ASSIGNMENTS

[NAME OF CLASS HERE]

Task List	Length of Time to Complete	Due Date
Reading assignment #___		
Reading assignment #___		
Reading assignment #___		
Reading assignment #___		
Reading assignment #___		
Special project		
Study for quiz		
Study for quiz		
Study for quiz		
Study for midterm		
Study for final		

APPLYING TO COLLEGES, FOR SCHOLARSHIPS, FOR INTERNSHIPS, ETC.

[NAME OF OPPORTUNITY HERE]

Task List	Length of Time to Complete	Due Date
Do research to identify opportunities		
Request application materials		
Select the colleges (or scholarships or internships) you are for applying to		
Write application essays		
Ask references if they'll write letters of recommendation		
Fill out application form		
Get copies of transcripts		
Follow up and collect letters of recommendation		
Get supplies (envelopes, stamps, photocopies, etc.)		
Submit applications		

PLANNING A SURPRISE PARTY FOR YOUR BEST FRIEND

Task List	Length of Time to Complete	Due Date
Make a guest list		
Make a supplies list		
Send Evites		
Shop for supplies		
Arrange for party decoy (the excuse you'll use to lure your unsuspecting friend to the party spot)		
Set up your playlist		
Decorate		

The Reality of Multitasking

When you've got more things to do than there are hours in the day, it's tempting to double or triple up on your tasks to fit it all in. I'm always doing a million things at once to make the most of my limited time and check off everything from my "to do" list (so I can create another one, of course). In just the past week, I've multitasked by:

- reading a research article while riding the bus downtown

- crocheting part of a baby blanket I was making as a gift while watching *American Idol*

- catching up on phone calls while waiting for a copy job to get finished at Kinko's

- dropping off letters at the post office while out for a run

- listening to a work-related podcast while walking my dog

How about you? Do you surf the web, watch TV, and text with a friend at the same time? Or study for your math quiz while listening to music, IM-ing your BFF, and catching up on your Instagram feed?

Even though I do it a lot, I'll be the first to admit that, while sometimes it's necessary, multitasking isn't always such a great thing. I'm all for efficient use of time, but when

multitasking becomes a way of life, it's easy to forget how to slow down and just "be in the moment." On top of that, relationships, friendships, and quality of work can actually suffer as a result of multitasking.

Opting to *not* multitask and instead concentrate on one thing at a time can result in more focused work and deeper quality time, and keep you from going into sensory overdrive. Before you multitask every last minute of your life away, don't forget to tune in to your emotional, mental, and physical needs and make sure that you're not neglecting any part of your life by giving it only half your focus (see Chapter 10 for more on tuning in).

Making Time Management Work for You

So . . . what do you say? Have I convinced you to give time management a shot and experience the stress-relieving results firsthand? Here are a few extra tips to keep in mind:

- **Be realistic** about how long each of your tasks will take, so you can create a plan that is achievable. (For example, don't budget a half hour to write a ten-page essay!) You might even want to consider building extra time into your plan in case something unexpected comes up.

- **Reward yourself** as incentive to keep moving forward and sticking to your schedule, especially when you're feeling burned out. (For example, for every hour of studying, give yourself five minutes to catch up on social media).

- **Be aware that procrastination and cramming only create more stress** than you'd be experiencing had you done the work along the way.

- **When planning your schedule, look into the future at least one month ahead** for big-picture perspective.

- **Don't forget to build time for yourself into your schedule!** Many busy business execs have their assistants schedule meetings with *themselves* just so they can have alone time to process and think. You deserve the same time, so take it!

Making It Stick

It may feel forced at first, but with a few simple tweaks to your routines, time management can become an organic way of life. Here are some suggestions for successfully incorporating it into your daily routine:

- **When it's time to get down to business, make sure you've got optimal work conditions.** Work takes a lot longer to do with the TV on, your Skype screen open, and your cell phone inches away (yes, even when it's on vibrate). The fewer distractions around, the more productive your work time will be.

- **Write the deadline into your calendar as soon as you get a new assignment,** and make a task list of the steps necessary for completing it.

- **Make a "to do" list** each morning (or the night before) of everything you hope to accomplish that day. Be realistic about what you can achieve, so that by the end of the day you feel on top of things instead of behind schedule. As you complete each task on your list, take great pleasure in crossing it off!

- **Don't forget to schedule hangout time with your friends.** Keeping your social life intact during high-stress times is key to maintaining balance in your life. By making friend time a priority and working it into your schedule, you'll be able to relax and enjoy yourself, rather than stressing over what else you should be doing instead of socializing. And when playtime is over, you'll be ready to focus on your work and not stress about having to sacrifice your social life.

- **Do a weekly "check in" with yourself.** Set aside time once a week to review your calendar or schedule and formulate a rough plan for what you hope to tackle that week. Use the time to review not only your calendar, but also your stress levels. Take stock of your physical, emotional, and mental well-being. Are your mind, body, and soul well balanced, or do you need to make adjustments in the weeks or months ahead?

JOURNAL IT:

- **Log your activities for a day.** You'll gain a lot of insight by discovering what you actually spend your time doing. Make a list in your journal of absolutely every activity or task you do in one day. Include things like  what you ate, what chores you did (from making your bed to taking out the garbage), where you went (to and from school and activities), and all the little details in between. You'll be amazed (and exhausted!) to see how much you already accomplish every day. Also make a note of how long various activities took you— it will be invaluable info down the road when you're creating time management plans.

- **Write about a time that you planned poorly** or didn't manage your time well. Explore where things went wrong and think about what you would do differently next time.

- **Write out a schedule for your dream day,** dream week, or dream month. If you could spend your time doing absolutely anything you wanted, how would you structure your life?

Quiz

Do you already practice good time management? Which answer feels most like something you'd do?

1. Your best friend is going through major drama with her boyfriend and has been texting you nonstop since you got home from school. Besides having to watch your little brother, you've got a ton of homework to do, but you hate leaving your friend in the lurch. You . . .

   a. *take a few minutes to plan out the rest of your evening and make a detailed list of everything you have to do, including getting back to your friend and giving her fifteen minutes of your undivided attention before hitting the books.*

b. *open your math book* and *grab your cell so you can start your homework while texting with your friend. Before you know it, you've blown an hour of your study time.*

2. It's Monday night, and you just realized you have three separate assignments due on Friday. You can't afford to flake out on any of them. You . . .

   a. *break down each assignment into mini-tasks and create a clear plan for completing each one over the next three days.*

   b. *decide to focus on one assignment from start to finish before giving the other two a second thought. Once you complete one, you can get started on the next. Hopefully, by the end of the week you'll have gotten it all done.*

3. It's your last chance to study before your final, but it's also the night of the two-hour season finale of your favorite show. You . . .

   a. *planned ahead and mapped out a study plan that includes a two-hour break so you can watch your show guilt free.*

   b. *were planning to TiVo your show so you could study, but you're so fried by the time your show starts that you ditch the study plans and reach for the remote.*

4. It's the first day of the semester, and each teacher gives you a syllabus highlighting future quiz and exam dates. You . . .

   a. *take your syllabi home that night and plug each and every important date into your calendar.*

b. *stick the syllabi in the back of your notebooks to look at some other time. You've got a grip on tomorrow's assignments . . . why worry about what's happening two months from now?*

5. Your mom's car is in the shop, so for the next week you'll be taking public transportation—forty-five minutes each way—back and forth to school. You . . .

a. *take advantage of your commute by using the time to catch up on required reading for each class. That way, when you get home, you'll already be ahead of schedule.*

b. *continually forget to charge your iPod or bring a book with you, and instead spend your commute annoyed with yourself for not taking advantage of the extra time.*

SCORING

Mostly As: You have a disciplined approach to planning and scheduling and have already established healthy time management habits.

Mostly Bs: You are more of a "fly by the seat of your pants" kind of gal. If that sometimes leaves you floundering when deadlines draw near, you might want to try a few time-management techniques.

CREATE YOUR OWN TIME MANAGEMENT AFFIRMATION

An affirmation is a positive statement you write or say to "affirm" or declare a way of thinking or being. Once you've come up with your affirmation, write it down on an index card or piece of paper and post it where you'll see it often. Use one of the examples below or create an affirmation of your own.

- *I have enough time to accomplish everything I need to get done.*

- *By organizing my time, I eliminate chaos and create balance in my life.*

- *I work efficiently by being organized and creating an ideal work environment.*

TIME WASTERS VS. CHILL TIME

When you're creating a plan for managing your time, don't forget to leave room for downtime, since it's oh-so-important to keeping your life in balance. But what's the difference between taking down time and just plain wasting time?

You're wasting time if you're:	You're taking downtime if you're:
Gossiping or listening to friends talk behind each other's back	Spending positive one-on-one time with a friend
Blowing an evening by scrolling through your various social media feeds	Updating your blog during a ten-minute study break
Checking your cell every two minutes while you study, and replying back immediately to anyone who texts you	Checking your cell once an hour for some quick catch-ups with friends
Procrastinating by flipping through all 834 channels to see what's on TV	Watching the results show on *American Idol* and then getting back to work
Sitting around all day on Saturday with no plans and no motivation	Catching a movie or taking advantage of the nice weather by going for a walk with a friend

Dear Debbie,

I know it's impossible to get rid of stress completely, but what's a way to balance it all out so it doesn't become so overpowering?

Stella, age 17

Dear Stella,

To stop stress from ruling your life, take back the power and get in control of your schedule. Come up with a strategy for juggling all the things going on in your life by figuring out how much time you need to get it all done and then planning how to set aside the time. Once you've come up with your plan, you can schedule in the stuff that's so important for keeping your life in balance, like alone time, family time, and hanging-out-with-friends time. Sometimes coming up with a plan of attack and sticking to it is all it takes. Good luck!

XOXO Debbie

TIME-OUT:
COLLEGE ADMISSIONS SURVIVAL GUIDE

College can be full of high drama, sleepless nights, and bundles of nerves. And that's before you even get there. If you've got college dreams, you know all too well about the stresses involved—trying to boost your GPA and class rank, participating in extracurriculars or volunteer work to show breadth on your  applications, scoring well on your standardized tests, writing strong essays, getting great recommendations, applying for scholarships, not to mention facing pressure from friends and family about where you should go, how you'll pay for it, and what you'll do with your degree when you're done. Phew . . . it's a lot to think about, to say the least.

While I don't have the answers for eliminating all of this anxiety, I do have some suggestions for making the process of applying to and getting into college more manageable.

Narrowing Down Your Options

- **Research, research, research.** Go online, go to a college fair, talk to your mentor, e-mail older friends who've already graduated and started college, and find out everything you can about your potential schools to get a true picture of what each school has to offer.

- To reduce stress about getting into your first choice, **apply to several schools,** making sure to include different types of schools and earmarking at least one as a fallback (but don't waste time applying to schools you truly don't want to go to).

- **Don't pressure yourself** about getting into "the" school. There is a school out there that will work well for you, even if it's not the one you were originally hoping for.

Handling Application Stress

- **Start researching colleges early** so you can be aware of any special application requirements (such as placement tests) you'll need to take care of before applying.

- Stay organized by making a **special basket or box for holding your college application materials.**

- **Make a timeline** of important application dates, factoring in all the important steps (getting transcripts and letters of recommendation, writing essays, and so on) and creating mini-deadlines for accomplishing each one. (For more on timelines, see Chapter 3.)

- **Give the people writing your letters of recommendation plenty of time** so they're more likely to say yes and write a fabulous letter.

- If some or all of the colleges you're applying to are members, **consider using the Common Application,** to save you time and energy by not duplicating your efforts. (www.commonapp.org)

- When writing your essay or essays, **be sure to outline before you start,** and give yourself ample time to draft and revise before completing your masterpiece.

- Take advantage of resources like **high school guidance counselors** for help in deciding which colleges to look into and which ones to apply to when narrowing down your list, as well as filling out applications.

Dealing with Parents

- Remember that **your parents are probably feeling pressure about your college applications too.** Try giving them a break, and hopefully they'll do the same for you!

- **Fill your parents in on your process** and approach for applying to college so they can see you're organized and have a plan for tackling it responsibly. This might help them nag less and focus their energy more usefully.

- When you're ready to apply, **present your parents with your plan** for the schools you're interested in. Be prepared to explain why you've selected the schools, since you'll need their support in helping you get there.

- **Give your parents specific tasks** so they can feel useful (plus, it will get them off your back for a while). Your parents would probably be happy to make photocopies and get mailing supplies ready, type up essays, or proofread your application materials. If they're trying to get involved where you don't need their help, approach them by saying something like, "Mom, please don't nag me about my essay . . . I'm still in the thinking stage. But once I put my thoughts on paper in the outline stage, I'd love to show it to you and get your feedback."

Dealing with Friends

- Depending on your friends' plans, talking about your application process might be uncomfortable or weird. Other times, talking about the process with someone who is going through the same thing might be exactly what you need to de-stress. To avoid college discussion burnout, **make a rule that certain hangout times are "college-free chat zones."**

- If friends are pressuring you about your college plans, **ask them to back off.** Let your friends know that while you appreciate their point of view, they can support you best by respecting your choices. Of course, maybe your friend is pressuring you because she really wants to talk about *her* decisions. You can help her de-stress by asking about and listening to what she's going through.

- If you're worried about losing touch with friends after going your separate ways, make plans to **start a private Facebook group or blog** where you can share pics and stories about your new lives.

Getting a Grip on Money Challenges

- **Ask your parents** and guidance counselor to help you negotiate the confusing hill of paperwork that's involved in applying for financial aid.

- Look for scholarship opportunities to help ease the financial burden—there's a lot of **free money out there** for people willing to do a little digging. (For more info, check out www.scholarships.com, www.scholarshiphelp.org, and www.fastweb.com.)

- **Work with your parents to come up with a plan** for paying for college. It would be a bummer to get into your top pick but have to pass because you can't make it work financially. If you're reading this book well before your senior year, talk to your parents early about how you and they plan to pay for college, and whether you should start getting summer jobs, save part of your allowance and birthday money from grandma, and so on.

Making the Final Choice

- If you get into more than one school and you're not sure where to go, **create a pro/con list for each of the schools** you're considering. (For more on making pro/con lists, see Chapter 5.)

- If you can, **visit each of the schools** you're considering. While you're on campus, tune in to your gut—can you imagine yourself thriving there?

- Since a lot of college application stress is anxiety over "making the wrong choice," put that anxiety into perspective by remembering that **with the right attitude you can have a great experience wherever you go.** (And if it seems like a bad fit, you can always transfer to another school down the road!)

CINEMATIC U.

Need to take a time-out from applications? Escape into Hollywood's version of collegiate life with one of these movies:

- *Good Will Hunting*
- *Old School*
- *Mona Lisa Smile*
- *Drumline*
- *Legally Blonde*
- *The Social Network*
- *Pitch Perfect*

For more info on surviving the college application process, visit the College Board online at www.collegeboard.org. This organization provides students with a ton of information on planning for, applying to, and paying for college. Good luck!

4

ORGANIZATION

How organized are you? Are the books on your shelves arranged in alphabetical order? Are the clothes in your closet divided into sections by season or color? Do you like it when everything has its place? Well, that's me. I'm drawn to files, folders, and three-ring binders like ants are to a picnic. Nothing excites me more than color-coding my notebooks or cleaning out my closet. (Okay, a giant pack of strawberry Twizzlers would come close.) Truth be told, my former coworkers called me "the chart queen" because of the obsessively designed (but practical, of course) Excel spreadsheets I made to track my work.

I wasn't always this way. In fact, I'm sure my mom is still floored every time she sets foot inside my office and realizes that her slob of a daughter—the one who slept many a night atop a pile of clothes strewn across the bed because she was too lazy to knock them onto the floor—has become an organization diva.

Organization diva. That has a nice ring to it, doesn't it? Well, you can be one too. For the overbooked, overscheduled teen, being organized is crucial. Think about it . . . doesn't magically finding an extra hour or two in your day sound good? Organization can do this. Being organized saves you time, which results in more freedom in your schedule, which leads to—you guessed it—less stress and more balance. So even if alphabetized, color-coded organization isn't your thing, have no fear—even a few small organizational shifts will lead to big results.

> **ORGANIZATION:** Instilling structure into your life with a goal of simplifying, creating order, and bringing peace to your everyday existence. Ideal for reducing stress related to:

- being overscheduled and overwhelmed
- feeling as though your life is full of chaos and disorder
- feeling swamped by the number of things on your plate
- completing assignments when up against tight deadlines
- never being able to find your favorite sweater, that book you borrowed from your sister's friend, or the birthday card you were going to mail to your favorite aunt

Why Organization Works

Have you ever been in class and reached into your book bag for your homework and come up empty-handed? Or maybe you went to shoot your lab partner an e-mail, but you couldn't track down his e-mail address anywhere. Maybe you were headed to a party with your friend when you realized you forgot the slip of paper where you scribbled down the address. Maybe you lugged all your research to the library so you could spend the day working on your term paper, but when you got started, you realized you left the outline requirements at home, so you had to turn around and head back.

These predicaments have one thing in common: *a little organization could have prevented each one.* When it comes to alleviating stress, organization can:

- **save you time** on homework and other assignments
- **prevent you from losing important information,** like class work, e-mail addresses, and other stuff
- **help you feel on top** of your workload, schedule, and social life
- **give you confidence** that you can get it all done
- **create less clutter in your life,** leaving more space for calm and serenity
- **give you a foundation for handling new stressors** that come your way

Organizing Your Life

Whether you want to become an official organization diva or just arrange your social life so you're not left high and dry with no plans on a Saturday night, here are some strategies for organizing the different areas of your life.

YOUR ROOM

No matter whether you share a tiny room with a sibling or you have a bedroom the size of a suite at the Plaza Hotel, the key to a peaceful and Zen home life is organization. If your room is messy and chaotic, chances are your life is going to feel that way too. By making some changes to bring more clarity into your living space, your life will follow suit. Creating structure out of your chaos—be it made up of shoes and clothing or schoolwork and books—doesn't have to take long or cost much. All you need is a will and a way. Here are some tips:

Purge, clear, and donate. All too many of us are addicted to hanging on to our "stuff." But do you really need those old ticket stubs or the single sock whose partner was last seen in the dryer six months ago? The first step to making your room a peaceful environment is to get rid of all the clutter (physical *and* emotional). Go through your closets, drawers, desktop, storage containers, and any other areas where "stuff" accumulates and examine each and every object. If too-small clothes from two seasons ago are taking up valuable closet space, set them aside to donate to a homeless shelter or Goodwill. If random newspapers, magazines, brochures, and school flyers are piling up, go through them, set aside what you want for keepsakes, and recycle the rest. To clear out emotional clutter, follow this rule of thumb: If you're keeping something you don't like out of a sense of obligation, or if looking at a particular item brings up bad memories and makes you feel icky, dump it!

Use bins, boxes, or baskets. Organize the various items in your room by grouping them and putting them into separate storage spaces. Old shoeboxes (free!) or plastic storage bins can be great for saving old artwork, school papers, and magazines, and can usually slide right under your bed. Small baskets on top of your desk can hold pens, pencils, staplers, and other desk supplies. Think creatively about how you can invent unique storage solutions by recycling—you probably already have many reusable containers (coffee tins, washed-out spaghetti sauce jars, etc.) at your fingertips.

Create a work space. You don't need a desk and chair in your bedroom to set aside a "work zone." Your work space can be as simple as a comfy pillow on the floor next to a wicker basket holding your school supplies. Keep a stock of blank notebooks or scrap paper (again, think recycle and use the blank side of old homework assignments), Post-its, and pens and pencils handy. If you do have a desk in your room, try to keep a small space—big enough to fit a piece of notebook paper—clear of clutter. Even if you use a computer for just about everything, having a little surface area for writing will add to the sense of neatness and order in your room.

Clean out your closet. You've got better things to do each morning than dig through your closet in search of the perfect outfit. Trim down your options by rotating your clothes each season—store bulky wool sweaters and cords in the basement or attic or in a sealed container under your bed during the summer, and keep shorts and tanks out of sight in the winter. To get rid of that three-foot-high pile of shoes on your closet floor, invest in a simple canvas or plastic shoe rack to hang on the inside of your closet door, or a few shoe shelves to keep pairs together. And if you haven't worn a pair of shoes in more than a year, consider moving it into storage or, better yet, donating it.

Make a bulletin board. I wanted lots of space to hang up
pics and articles when I was in high school, so my dad covered half my wall with corkboard and burlap, making one giant bulletin board. Even if you don't go to that extreme, you might consider picking up a small corkboard and some tacks from your local hardware store or painting your wall with magnetic paint so you can post reminders, important dates, favorite pictures . . . whatever inspires you!

YOUR LOCKER

Admittedly, most of the time my high school locker doubled as a tall, slender garbage can. I'd swing by it between classes to dump off any books and papers I could and let the pileup begin. At the end of the day, I'd inevitably find myself rooting through my locker in search of an elusive binder or a loose homework assignment, which almost always left me frustrated and with no option but

to sort through every sticky object in my search. Sound familiar? Then get to school early one day and spend fifteen minutes transforming your locker from dump to five-star resort.

Throw out trash. This probably goes without saying, but toss out or recycle any and all loose papers, food wrappers, crumpled notes, spent tissues, and other trash taking up valuable real estate. And make a vow to walk the extra fifty feet to the trash can the next time you're tempted to use your locker as a garbage receptacle.

Separate things for home. If you've got a shelf inside your locker, place items that you need to bring home with you that night on the shelf as the day goes by, so when the last bell rings, you've already set aside the important stuff.

Post reminders. Treat the inside of your locker like a mini bulletin board. Post memos about upcoming tests, notes about things to do, and countdowns for big events like finals or sports tournaments. You'll be reminded, motivated, and inspired every time you dial your locker combination.

YOUR COMPUTER FILES

Your computer desktop is great for showcasing favorite screen savers or rotating pics of your nearest and dearest. But if you're like many people, you end up storing a ton of documents there too, turning your desktop into a virtual junkyard. There are two problems with this technological disarray: (1) parking old documents on your desktop adds to computer clutter, ultimately making it harder to quickly find the important stuff, and (2) storing a lot of files on your desktop actually slows down your computer. The solution? Implement a simple filing system on your computer.

Create folders. First, create folders on your hard drive called "My Documents," "My Music," and "My Photos." Then, within those folders, create one folder for each of the big themes in your life (School, Volunteering, Friends, Favorites, Writing) and then make subfolders within each of those. For example, your "School" folder might have subfolders for each school year, and within each school year folder, you might have a folder for each class. The more detailed your filing system, the more likely you'll always be able to track down important info when you need it.

Create a system for naming your documents, images, and audio files, so you can easily find them when you're tracking things down. For example, you might consider naming all your class notes the same way, such as "Biology Lecture Notes [insert date]" or "Comp Assignment [insert name]" and so on.

Update files monthly. When things get really busy, it's all too easy to save time by dumping new docs onto your desktop or creating new, random folders. Once a month, set aside a half hour to dive into your hard drive and put everything where it belongs. File away scattered, loose files and create new subfolders if you need to.

Delete when you can. If you're holding on to extra-large files like videos, delete them from your computer once you've exported them to YouTube or Vimeo so they don't take up valuable memory and slow down your computer. If you can't bear to dump them, consider storing them on an external hard drive or on a hosting site like MediaFire.

YOUR E-MAIL IN-BOX

Do you have a hard time staying on top of your e-mail in-box? Tracking down important messages, finding elusive e-mail addresses, and searching for pictures, assignments, and other attachments can be overwhelming if you don't have a system for organizing your virtual mailbox.

No matter what e-mail program you use, organizing your in-box can save you oodles of time. Here are some suggestions:

Create mail folders. Most mail programs allow users to set up "folders," "mailboxes," or "labels" for filing away e-mails. Since there's no cap on the number of mail folders you can have, create one for every part of your life: personal keepsakes, passwords, homework, jokes, classes, colleges, and so on. As soon as you've read a new e-mail and taken the necessary action (replying, forwarding, etc.), move it out of your in-box and file it away for easy access and safekeeping.

Manage your sent items. Many of us use our "Sent Items" folder as a way to track every e-mail that's come from us. Not a bad plan, except that in no time, you may have hundreds of e-mails taking up valuable space, and if your Sent Items folder gets too full, your mail program could slow down to a crawl, or your computer may have a problem opening or indexing the file and you may lose messages. The solution? As soon as you send an e-mail (or at the end of each day or week), go to your Sent folder and decide whether or not you want to keep the message. If you do, file it away in the appropriate folder (see above), and if not, move it straight to the trash.

Save attachments. When you receive an e-mail with an attachment (or attachments), click on "Save Attachment" and then delete the message. To simplify this even further, you could create a folder called "Saved Attachments" so all your attachments will be stored in the same place.

Delete junk. One of the best ways to keep your e-mail in-box clean is to delete items as soon as you're done with them. Junk mail? *Delete.* Bad joke e-mails? *Delete.* Announcements about events that already happened? *Delete.* (Did I mention that pushing the delete button can be incredibly fun . . . or is it just me who feels this way?)

Flag important items. Most e-mail programs give you the option of marking or flagging important items. If you have an important e-mail you'll need to deal with down the road, mark it with a flag or star. (Just be sure you don't flag *everything* in your in-box, or the symbol will lose its impact.)

YOUR VIRTUAL LIFE

Organizing your virtual life can be a complicated proposition if you have multiple devices and no single one is ever completely up-to-date. The solution? The cloud.

Choose a cloud calendar. Keep track of all your important dates on a cloud calendar like Google or iCloud, and download the associated free app for each device. Then, update your settings so that the calendars automatically and frequently sync to one another.

Sync your smart phone. Regularly sync your smart phone with your computer to make sure all your valuable info—photos, contacts, and so on—are backed up and live in more than once place.

YOUR SCHOOLWORK

When you've got a heavy workload littered with assignments, quizzes, and other school tasks, an organized approach will go a long way toward helping you meet your deadlines with as little stress as possible. Being organized will also help you be more efficient and reduce the chances you'll have to redo your work. Here are some tips:

Organize by class. Use a separate notebook or folder for each class, or dedicate a different section of your three-ring binder to each. If you can, find notebooks or binders with a pocket on the inside cover to store your reading list, syllabus, and any other handouts. When taking lecture notes, mark the date and the subject on the top of the page so you can easily find your material when it's study time.

Create folders for big assignments. When it's project time, store any and all info having to do with your assignment—research, notes, handouts, phone numbers of classmates—inside a dedicated pocket folder or manila envelope.

Make a homework tracker. Keep track of all your assignments, big and small, in a small notepad or notebook, or use an app or online system specifically designed to help you track your tasks. If you're doing it on paper, divide each page into three columns: one for the name of the class, one for the assignment, and one for the deadline. Once you've completed an assignment, cross it out. (For more on keeping track of assignments, see Chapter 3 on time management.)

If you've ever written a major paper for a class, you know that keeping all your sources straight, ideas flowing, and deadlines met can be a tremendous feat. Here are some tried-and-true tips for organizing your term papers or class projects:

Organize with index cards. Before you start writing, buy a stack of index cards (or you can cut plain paper into small rectangles) and use each card to represent one idea or concept that you want to include in your paper. Brainstorm and be as thorough as possible in creating your cards—there's no limit to the number you can make, and it's better to have more ideas than fewer at this point. Once you're finished, spread out the index cards on a flat surface (the dining room table, your bedroom floor), and group the ideas and concepts together into broad themes. Then rearrange each pile of themed cards, placing them in a logical order. Voilà . . . you now have the ingredients for your outline.

Keep research records. As you pore through magazines, books, and websites researching your project, create a "one-sheet" for each source you take notes on. At the top of the one-sheet, note the name of the source (such as the title of the book, or the name of the magazine and article), where you found it (a website address), the author, the date it was written, and any other details you'll eventually need for your bibliography. The rest of the one-sheet should be your notes from the source or quotes that you'll be using in your paper or project.

Keep electronic drafts. Keep every draft of your paper on your computer or in a hard copy, at least until the assignment has been turned in and graded. As you edit your project, you might delete material that could be useful in a redraft or for a future assignment. You did the work—don't throw it away until you're sure you won't be using it!

YOUR SOCIAL LIFE

Life is so hectic that when you do have a chance to chill out with friends, there's nothing worse than blowing your opportunity by spending all day trying to figure out what to do. That's right . . . even your social life could benefit from a little organization.

Schedule regular "girls' nights out." Come up with a regular time (monthly or weekly) for catching up with your girlfriends—like movie nights every other Friday, once-a-month pedicure dates, Sunday-morning jogs in the park—so you don't have to stress about when you're going to catch up next.

Trade Spaces with a friend (for a day). A fresh take on reorganizing your room might result in all kinds of creative solutions for a more peaceful and productive personal space. Grab a friend, have a good laugh over your third-grade class photos, and organize your room at the same time. Then tackle your friend's room the following weekend!

Making It Stick

So are you ready to get organized and stay that way? Here are some suggestions for making the new organized you a permanent fixture:

- **Dedicate one morning a month to clearing your clutter.** Purge, organize, and recycle, and you'll start off each month feeling on top of everything in your life. Plus, it's the perfect thing to do on a rainy day!

- **Buy a few office supplies** or ask your parents or teachers if they have any old supplies you can reuse. Setting up systems of organization using simple items like file folders, envelopes, baskets, or plastic bins can go a long way in converting your mess from stress to Zen . . . for good.

JOURNAL IT:

- **Write out your short- and long-term organizational goals.** Make your goals as specific as possible, and brainstorm the steps you'll need to take in order to accomplish them. For example: **Goal**—*Prevent a last-minute scramble when putting together the bibliography for my term paper.* **How to Achieve Goal**—*Make a folder to keep all my original research in, and make sure I note any source information the second I find a new article to include.*

- **Think about an area of your life where your lack of organization causes you stress.** Now visualize how you'd like this area of your life to flow based on a more organized you. Then answer these questions in your journal: *What does it look like to be organized? How does it feel to be so organized? What changes do I need to make for this vision to become a reality?*

Are you an organized person? Look at the scenarios below and see which one feels most like you:

1. On any given day, your bedroom . . .

   a. *looks like it was just hit by a cyclone.*

   b. *could be presentable with just a five-minute pickup.*

   c. *would pass the white glove dust test.*

2. Your school locker . . .

   a. *has a foot-high pile of "stuff" on the bottom that hasn't seen the light of day in months.*

   b. *isn't at risk for an avalanche, but could use an interior designer.*

   c. *is clean enough to eat a meal out of.*

3. When you reach into your backpack to find a pen, you just might pull out . . .

   a. *last week's half-eaten banana.*

   b. *a handful of notebooks and some crumpled tissues.*

   c. *a pack of multicolored pens . . . one for each class.*

4. Your school notebooks . . .

   a. *are full of blank pages, since you rarely take notes in them.*

   b. *contain fairly legible notes, along with some doodles in the margins.*

c. *are color-coded and streaked with highlighters.*

5. Your bedroom closet . . .

a. *resembles the dressing room at Macy's after a busy Saturday afternoon.*

b. *is generally pretty neat, unless it's recovering from a recent wardrobe crisis.*

c. *is as neat as Oprah's (even if it is only a fraction of the size).*

SCORING

Mostly As: Hate to say it, but you're a bit of a slob—life might run more smoothly if you introduced a little organization into the mix.

Mostly Bs: You prefer order over chaos but can go with the flow when life intervenes.

Mostly Cs: You're super organized . . . just make sure you don't stress over the occasional mess!

CREATE AN ORGANIZATION AFFIRMATION

Write down your affirmation on an index card or piece of paper and post it where you'll see it often. Use one of the examples below or create an affirmation of your own.

- *I am an organized person with a place for everything I need in my life.*

- *By clearing my clutter, I create a more calm and peaceful environment.*

- *I have a structure in place for handling any new stressors that come my way.*

TIPS FROM AN EXPERT

To get some organization tips from a pro, I chatted with **Lisa Viscardi**, an organizational consultant through her company, Clarity, and the cofounder of Lunchopolis, the garbage-free lunchbox.

Me: Why is being organized so important for teens looking to reduce their stress and find balance?

Lisa: When your environment is chaotic and hard to manage, it increases the stress in your life. Conversely, when you keep your environment in order, it helps create space for you to relax. It's all about clarity. "Clarity" means clear. When your living environment is clear, *you're* clear, and it's only when you're clear that you can truly relax and restore.

Me: What's one organizational "tool" that would help every teen organize her life?

Lisa: The most important thing I teach people is to keep everything that they need to get done, or their "to do's," all in one place. Since the biggest "to do's" for teens are most likely school-related, try to keep your homework neatly on your desk in folders, or get a cool basket to keep your folders in, and you will always know where your work is.

Here are Lisa's tips for girls looking to organize their rooms, their schoolwork, or their social lives:

- *Get rid of stuff.* If you don't love it, you don't really need it. (This can be true about friends, too, but that's a whole other story!) There are many charities who would love to get your old stuff to give to teens who have less than you do.

- *Keep everything that is the same together.* This may sound obvious, but so many people don't do it. Put your jeans with jeans, books with books, jewelry with jewelry, and so on.

- *Make a place for everything.* When you go to put your stuff away, you'll know where to put it and, more important, where to find it.

- *Spend a few minutes each night cleaning up your room* and getting everything you need ready for the next day. Those few minutes will help you go to sleep more peacefully and ease into the morning much more effortlessly.

- *Create an environment on the outside that reflects how you want to feel inside.*

- *Don't procrastinate.* Believe it or not, straightening up takes very little time—it's really about making the effort. Bottom line, you will feel much calmer in your life if you clarify your space.

Dear Debbie,

I was pressured to apply to top-notch colleges, but I know that I need a small, less rigorous school in order to thrive. I also didn't want to go very far away from home, but friends and family were urging me to take a bigger step. How can I keep from getting totally stressed out while I'm figuring out which school is the perfect choice for me?

Cassandra, age 18

Dear Cassandra,

There's no doubt that choosing which college to attend is a major life decision, so you're right to put a lot of thought into it. Start out by gathering all the info you can on each school and create folders for all your material and research. When it comes time to narrow down your choices, take an organized approach. Grab a stack of index cards, and on each one, write down a factor that is important to you when it comes to making your decision, being as thorough as possible. For example, one index card might read "driving distance from home," another might read "small class sizes," and so on. Once you have your cards ready, go through them one by one. If a contender for college fits the criteria, jot down that name on the card and then do this for every card and every school. When you're done, you should notice that one or two schools most closely fit your criteria, and you'll be that much closer to making your final decision. You'll also have helpful "research" to show your parents why you made your choice, especially useful if they're not initially on board with your chosen school. Hopefully, they'll be impressed with your conscientious decision-making approach and will switch gears and support you. Good luck at school next year!

XOXO Debbie

5

SPEAKING UP
AND SAYING NO

Do you constantly put other people's needs ahead of your own? Are you overly concerned with making sure the people in your life are happy? Do you often say yes to things you'd rather say no to in an attempt to avoid hurting someone's feelings or letting somebody down—or out of a sense of guilt, obligation, or insecurity? Then you might be what's known as a "people pleaser," or you may just be like many people who find saying no extremely challenging.

I mean, who doesn't cringe at the thought of being seen as negative, difficult, or confrontational? But what you may not realize is that saying yes to something you don't want to do builds up negative energy in the form of frustration and annoyance, both for you and the other people involved. And it goes without saying that it creates more stress in your life.

It's time to learn how to speak up for yourself. You just might find that not only is it easier than you thought, but also, by saying a few truthful sentences, you can very quickly simplify your overscheduled life and let go of unwanted stress.

SAYING NO AND SPEAKING UP: Being honest with yourself and everyone else about your thoughts, feelings, and ideas, and making choices that are in your best interest. Ideal for reducing stress related to:

- having friends place demands on you and your time

- being overscheduled and overbooked

- trying to determine which extracurricular activities and social opportunities to be a part of

- feeling pressure to make your parents happy

It's such a simple concept. Too many things on your plate? Totally overbooked? Just eliminate some of your commitments! But as is the case with many things in life, *easier said than done*. When you're busy trying to beef up your extracurriculars in order to be competitive on college applications, not to mention live up to your parents' and teachers' and *your own* expectations, sometimes you might forget *you actually have a choice in the matter*.

Why Saying No and Speaking Your Truth Is Tough

Why do people get caught up in this cycle of saying yes and overcommitting themselves in the first place? Maybe it's because most people are:

- afraid of missing out on a great opportunity (aka FOMO)

- concerned they won't be seen as impressive to other people

- worried that saying no will be considered a sign of weakness

- full of guilt at the thought of letting other people down

- anxious about hurting people's feelings or offending them

- not very good at putting their own needs first

I know that in a world where *doing more* and *being more* are often valued above all else, saying no to an opportunity can be a frightening proposition. But it doesn't have to be. Learning to speak your truth and say no when you need to can be an incredibly empowering (and freeing) thing.

I used to be super concerned about how other people felt when it came to what I was doing and the choices I made. In fact, I was so concerned about how my actions might affect others that most of the time I forgot to consider how they made *me* feel. What I discovered is that it's utterly *exhausting* to always put other people's needs first, especially when you realize this very important fact: *You can't control how other people feel or think about the things you do. The only person whose thoughts and emotions you can control is you.* Even if you spent every minute of every day trying to please other people, they still might not be any happier or appreciate you any more. Once I had this *aha* moment, choosing *me* became much easier.

Don't get me wrong—I'm not saying that you shouldn't care about other people's feelings or how your actions affect others. I'm saying that your number one priority when it comes to making healthy choices—choices to keep you sane, happy, peaceful, and balanced—needs to be *you*.

Finding Your Voice

So how do you know when you're doing something for the wrong reasons? Here are three different techniques you can use, together or separately, to help you make smart choices that can reduce your stress:

1. Create a mission statement.

2. Weigh the pros and cons.

3. Tune in to your gut.

CREATING A MISSION STATEMENT

Back when I was trying to figure out what to do with my life, a friend encouraged me to write a mission statement for myself. At the time, the idea seemed pretty out there. Weren't mission statements something companies used to describe their business approach, goals, and strategies? What did that have to do with my dream of writing for a living?

Despite my hesitation, I took a stab at it and asked myself, *If I were a company, what would my mission be?* Here's what I came up with:

> My mission is to be involved in creating media that inspires and empowers women and girls to live more fulfilling lives and be the best they can be.

Okay. I had the mission statement. Now what? Well, the "what" became clear as I moved forward in my career and life. Suddenly I had a measure for figuring out which opportunities to seize and which to pass on. All I had to do was go back to what I wrote and ask the question, *Does this opportunity fit in* *with my mission statement goals or distract from them?*

Does writing a mission statement make sense for you? You might want to give it a try if you find yourself constantly:

- taking on more than you can comfortably handle

- having a hard time prioritizing your extracurricular activities

- feeling like you need to cut back on your obligations

Fear not . . . you don't need to know exactly what you want to do or even have a clear, concrete goal in mind to write a mission statement, and since it can change right along with you, there's no need to put pressure on yourself to create the "perfect" statement now. Here are some ideas for what your own mission statement might look like:

- My mission is to be involved in activities that allow me to contribute something to society.

- My mission is to pursue my dream of being a [insert career dream here] someday because it's important that I [insert why you want to do it here].

- My mission is to be the best [insert sport here] player I can be.

- My mission is to put my best academic effort forward so I can get into my dream college someday.

Write out a mission statement for yourself here:

_____

_____

Now that you have your mission statement, use it the next time you want to make a smart choice by answering these questions:

1. Does this opportunity fit in with my mission statement goals?

2. Does this activity improve my chances of reaching my goals?

3. Will cutting back on this activity negatively impact my ability to reach my goals?

Then look at your answers and see which choice makes the most sense for you!

WEIGHING THE PROS AND CONS

You may already use this straightforward method in your life without even realizing it, since our minds have a way of weighing the pros and cons of a situation or choice almost subconsciously. Here's how it works. For every choice you need to make—from how to clear out or beef up your schedule to figuring out the best way to handle a messy social situation—weigh the pros (upsides) and cons (downsides) of your various options. In most cases, whichever option has the most pros wins (see page 80 for an exception to this rule).

Here are two examples of how the pro/con approach could work for two very different situations.

The Choice: Whether or Not to Audition for the Spring Musical

PROS	CONS
I love the musical they're doing this year!	If I make it, rehearsals could interfere with volleyball practice.
I'll meet new people outside my normal social group.	Some of my friends think being in the musical is lame.
I love to sing and act.	If I don't get in, I'll be totally bummed.
I've always had a great time doing musicals in the past.	
It's another thing to put on my résumé.	
I'll get to travel to the County Theater Festival.	
There's always downtime at rehearsals for studying.	
My BFF is trying out too, so we could do it together.	

In this example, there are definitely more pros than cons, and since no one pro or con clearly outweighs the other (unless volleyball is the most important thing in your life), the choice here is pretty obvious—*go for it*. But here's another example where the choice isn't as cut and dry:

**The Choice: Whether or Not to Pursue
Your Crush from Spanish Class**

PROS	CONS
He's cute and nice.	He's already dating my best friend.
He seems to be interested in me.	
I could have a date for prom.	
He's good at Spanish, and could help me study.	
We'd look really great together.	
He's the perfect guy for me.	

While the pros definitely outnumber the cons here, the one con is a biggie—pretty much outweighing the sum of everything on the left side and more. (Of course, if you were in this situation, hopefully your choice would be evident without having to make these lists in the first place!)

If weighing the pros and cons is a new concept to you, why not give it a try the next time you're faced with a tough decision? Whether you're deciding if you want to try out for cross-country, or are considering blowing your savings on a Marc Jacobs bag, weighing the pros and cons will put some perspective on your indecision angst.

Have you ever been in a place or situation where something wasn't quite right? Maybe you didn't feel safe, or there was something going on that made you feel uneasy. Or maybe there was a person or group of people in your immediate environment that you didn't trust. For reasons you couldn't pinpoint—some kind of a "sixth sense"—you didn't feel comfortable in the situation. It's smart to pay attention to that powerful sensation.

To some people it's *intuition*, to others it's a *hunch*. I like the phrase *gut instinct*. Whatever you want to call it, you should listen when your subconscious has a strong sense about something you should or shouldn't do, what's best for you, or something going on that you need to be aware of. Some people notice these gut instincts more easily than others, but that's just because they know how to tap into this hidden gift. If you can learn how to tune in to your gut, you'll discover you actually do know what to do when facing tough and stressful situations.

When you first begin tuning in, you'll find it often takes a conscious effort and lots of practice to connect with and listen to your body's sixth sense. Here's a four-step process to make it a little easier: *ask*, *wait*, *listen*, and *trust*.

- **ASK questions.** If you're trying to figure out how to handle an opportunity or situation, put the question out to the "universe." Close your eyes and ask (out loud or to yourself): *Is _____ the right choice for me to make right now? Is _____ exciting or interesting to me? Am I considering this choice out of a sense of guilt or because I am feeling pressure to do so?*

- **WAIT and be patient.** Even your gut sometimes takes a while to make the right choice in a difficult situation, so don't expect instant results. The answer will eventually come to you.

- **LISTEN to your body.** Sometimes your body gives *very* clear signals about what feels like the wrong or right choice. If the thought of being involved in a particular activity or taking a specific action makes you feel sick to your stomach or a general "heaviness" in your heart, mind, and body, your gut is saying it's not the right choice. Likewise, a feeling of lightness and joy is usually a good indicator of a positive choice.

- **TRUST your instinct.** If after tuning in to your gut you get a clear answer, make your choice and trust in yourself that you made the right decision, even if it is a difficult or uncomfortable one. Try not to second-guess yourself. Trust in the process and in the decision you made by letting your gut lead the way.

GETTING THE WORDS OUT

Okay. Now you know how to get clear on what your voice has to say, but how do you translate that to the outside world, especially if you've got to say "no" to someone else?

The solution is simple: *you speak up*. Easier said than done, I know, especially if you're someone who isn't quite comfortable letting others down. But unless you vocalize what you want, you're likely going to stay stuck in the same stressful, dissatisfied place you were before. We're going for *less* stress here, not more, so follow these four steps to get the words out:

- **Get clear on your intention.** Remind yourself *why* you're making this change. You're not trying to disappoint or screw someone else—you're making a choice that you know is best for your personal well-being. And what could be wrong with that?

- **Rehearse the scene.** Script out exactly what you want to say. You don't have to give excuses or even go into detail explaining your decision. A simple, "This isn't the best place for me to put my energy right now" or "I've decided I really need to focus on X right now" is just fine.

- **Speak up.** Say the words you planned confidently and clearly. It might be scary or feel uncomfortable, but getting the words out becomes easier with practice. I promise.

- **Be okay with what they say.** Remember that you can't control how others will feel or respond to your news. It's okay for them to be disappointed—it doesn't mean you're doing the wrong thing, even if your news isn't what they wanted to hear.

Making It Stick

Becoming comfortable with saying no and speaking up for yourself can take some getting used to, but following these guidelines will give you the confidence to put your needs first in a positive and healthy way.

- Remember that the only person who can make the right choice for you is you.

- **Know that putting yourself first and saying no will get easier the more you do it.**

- **It's impossible to do everything well**—put your energy into the things that inspire and excite you the most.

- **When you eliminate from your schedule the activities that don't inspire you,** you'll find more joy in the ones you continue participating in.

- **Avoid situations that make you feel stress,** and become aware of people who place unnecessary and unrealistic expectations or demands on you and your time. The only person whose needs you can fulfill is you.

JOURNAL IT:

- **Make a list of everything you have going on in your life,** including extracurricular activities, classes, jobs, and family responsibilities. Go through each item on your list and do a "gut tune-in." Take note of anything on your list that your "gut" feels is adding unnecessary stress to your life and you'd be better off without.

- **Write about a time you said yes to something you really wanted to say no to,** and explore the situation by answering these questions: *Why do you think you said yes in the first place? How did you feel while you were in the situation having said yes? What do you think would have happened if you had spoken your*

truth and passed on the opportunity from the start?
How would you do things differently next time?

Quiz

Do you know how to put your own needs first, speak up, and
say no when you need to?

1. You get a text message from your best friend begging
    you to go dress shopping after school for the spring
    formal. You were planning to head straight home to
    put the finishing touches on your semester-long science
    project due tomorrow, so you tell her you'd love to help
    but it will have to be another time.

    No . . . I'd probably give in (0 points)

    Depends on my mood (1 point)

    Yeah, that's me (2 points)

2. Your mom has been pushing you to try out for
    cheerleading, partly because she used to be a
    cheerleader and partly because her best friend's
    daughter is on the squad. Cheerleading hasn't been
    on your radar, and you're already double booked with
    debate team and yearbook, so you break the news to
    Mom that cheerleading's not in your future.

    No . . . I'd probably give in (0 points)

    Depends on my mood (1 point)

    Yeah, that's me (2 points)

3. You've put together a challenging schedule for the fall, including one AP class and two honors classes. A spot in AP English just opened up, and the teacher, one of your faves, encourages you to join the class. You know one more AP class would push you over the edge, so you thank her for thinking of you and tell her you'll see her next semester.

> *No . . . I'd probably give in (0 points)*
>
> *Depends on my mood (1 point)*
>
> *Yeah, that's me (2 points)*

4. You're a self-proclaimed volunteer junkie, so when an opportunity arises to take a day off from school to clean up a park, you feel conflicted about what to do. Ultimately, you turn down the opportunity, since you're already volunteering with the local preschool, and though you want to help protect the environment, cleaning up the park doesn't further your mission of working with children.

> *No . . . I'd probably give in (0 points)*
>
> *Depends on my mood (1 point)*
>
> *Yeah, that's me (2 points)*

5. Your schedule is packed—jazz band, student council, soccer, volunteer work, and a heavy course load—but your best friend is trying to rope you into running with her for class office. You feel confident that together you could probably win, and it would look great on your college applications, but running for office isn't something you've ever really wanted to do. You wish

your friend good luck and encourage her to find another running mate.

No . . . I'd probably give in (0 points)

Depends on my mood (1 point)

Yeah, that's me (2 points)

SCORING

How'd you do? Add up your points to find out.

0–3 points: You have a hard time speaking up for yourself and saying no, even when you know it's the better choice for you. To build your confidence, try saying no when the stakes aren't so high and experience how good it feels to speak your truth.

4–7 points: Some situations are harder than others when it comes to standing up for yourself and saying no. Remember to put your own needs first and be honest with yourself about what you want to do.

8–10 points: You know your strengths and limitations very well and are extremely self-interested. If you continue to make smart choices by weighing the options and tuning in, you'll be on your way to feeling balanced and fulfilled.

CREATE A "SPEAKING YOUR TRUTH" AFFIRMATION

Write it down on an index card or piece of paper and put it where you'll see it often. Here are a few ideas to get you started:

- *I make choices that bring balance and joy into my life.*

- *When I stand up for myself, I always make the right decisions.*

- *Sometimes saying no to an opportunity is actually saying yes to me.*

WHAT ANNEMARIE DOES

"I'm a horrible procrastinator, so I often find myself in a self-induced stressful state. When things get really busy, I take a good look at my calendar and reschedule all nonessential work, personal, and social appointments. If they don't serve to relieve my stress and only add to it, they are off!" —AnneMarie Kane, marketing & communications executive

Dear Debbie,

How do I handle things like problems at home and school if I'm too shy to deal most of the time?

Emily, age 12

Dear Emily,

I can see how being shy and having a hard time speaking up can be a problem when you're faced with stressors in your home and school life. First, know that you're not alone in being shy—half of us struggle with shyness about something. Second, know that you can overcome your shyness with a little practice. When you're struggling with a situation that requires you to speak up for yourself, plan ahead what you're going to say and practice it over and over so you can get comfortable saying the words. You might even try role-playing the scene with a friend. You may not reach a point where you feel 100 percent comfortable speaking up, but it will get easier with time. Hang in there, and good luck finding your voice!

XOXO Debbie

TIME-OUT:
GOTTA WORK? FINDING BALANCE WHEN YOU HAVE A JOB

Do you have a part-time job? Approximately sixteen percent of high school students in the United States spend evenings and/or weekends doing things like flipping burgers, popping popcorn, and ringing up sales for cash. Some teens work because they have to help their family make ends meet, while others are saving for a car or college or want to have spending money for going out with friends.

Whatever your reason for working, there's no doubt that having a job presents its own challenges for teens trying to keep their hectic lives in balance. So here are some tips for doing just that:

- **Be honest.** Trying to do a job you're not qualified for is guaranteed to add more stress to your life. When you're interviewing for a job, be honest about your experience and your skill set. (For example, if you've never babysat before, you may not be ready for a job at a daycare.)

- **Be aware.** When your schoolwork peaks in intensity, the last thing you need is to lose twenty hours at the hot dog stand in the mall. Since managers usually create work schedules two weeks ahead of time, give your manager any requested days off as soon as you know them. Even better, type up a list of your no-work days or weeks and turn them in to your manager at the beginning of the semester after you get your course syllabi. Be sure to keep a copy of your written request in the event your boss doesn't stick to his or her word.

- **Be friendly.** Get to know the people you work with and exchange phone numbers in case you need a last-minute shift switch to accommodate an unexpected assignment or other crisis. Let your work friend know to call you if she finds herself in a jam too . . . she'll be more likely to help you out when you need it if you're there for her as well. Plus, being friends with your coworkers will make time fly on the job!

- **Be realistic.** When you're thinking with your wallet and not your head, it's tempting to ask for more hours, especially if you're saving for something you really want. Be careful not to overcommit yourself, and be realistic about the number of hours you can work without other areas of your life (schoolwork, sports, and personal time) suffering. (For tips on budgeting your time, see Chapter 3.)

- **Be happy.** If you're going to spend fifteen or twenty hours a week at a part-time job, you owe it to yourself to make sure it's time well spent. Do you cringe at the thought of interacting with strangers? Then being a hostess at a restaurant probably isn't the best fit. Can't stand wearing uniforms? Then cross fast-food joint off your list of potential jobs. The point is, don't settle for a job you don't enjoy . . . life's too short!

LOOKING
OUT

6

CREATING A
SUPPORT SYSTEM

Ever feel like you're expected to do it all—succeed in school, have amazing friends, look fabulous, have a flawless family, find the best after-school job, get into the right college, and land the lead role in the class play, all while having an upbeat, go-get-'em attitude and never breaking a sweat? Oh yeah . . . I almost forgot. The above-mentioned feats should be accomplished single-handedly. After all . . . isn't asking for help the same thing as admitting you're not perfect?

Talk about *stress*.

The Beatles got it right in their song, "With a Little Help from My Friends." Everyone, including you, could benefit from having their own personal support system of family and friends to give advice, share a different perspective, and help out when things get challenging. Because the truth is, asking for help isn't a sign of weakness at all . . . it's a sign of *strength*.

You don't have to be in the midst of a crisis to appreciate the support of people who care about you either. In fact, by having a strong foundation of support in place, you'll be less likely to allow stresses to become full-fledged crises.

ASKING FOR HELP: Acknowledging that you could use help and reaching out to the people in your life for support. Ideal for reducing stress related to:

- figuring out how to prioritize your workload

- feeling like you're constantly deflecting peer pressure

- staying safe in stressful circumstances

- feeling ostracized by friends

- being bullied or harassed at school, in your neighborhood, or at a job

- worrying about physical concerns such as obesity, STDs, pregnancy, eating disorders, or addiction

When to Ask for Help

We've already determined that pretty much everyone is stressed out to the max. So when is it time to suck it up and deal on your own versus reaching out to your support system? While you don't have to be going through a challenge to lean on your friends, don't ignore any of these stress symptoms, as they're strong indicators that your body and soul are in need of outside life support:

- You feel overwhelmed a lot of the time.

- You're so stressed out that you have trouble sleeping at night.

- When you do find the time to buckle down and study, you're unable to concentrate.

- Your appetite has disappeared or you find you're bingeing in an attempt to relieve your stress.

- You're crying more than usual or are feeling sad a lot of the time.

If you're experiencing any of these symptoms, it's clear you could benefit from the support and insight of those around you. So brush off your pride, put your well-being first, and ask for what you need.*

* NOTE: If any of these symptoms is persistent or getting worse, it's time to seek the help of professionals who know just how to give you what you need. See page 131 for more information.

Where to Find Help

If you take a minute to look around—at your school, at home, and in your community—you'll likely find a whole slew of people already in place, just waiting for you to come to them with your stressful situation. Here are some suggestions for building up your support network.

PARENTS AND SIBLINGS

You might overlook your parents as a helpful resource for obvious reasons—it's all too easy to assume they don't have a clue about your reality. I mean, it *has* been a while since they were teenagers. But you might be surprised to discover that, clueless though they may be, your parents would be more than eager to help, if only they knew what you needed. Let's face it, your parents have a lot of experience when it comes to juggling it all—they've raised a family, balanced checkbooks, and held jobs, all at the same time. Just the fact that they've made it this far in life gives them serious cred. To get them on board, set aside a time to talk with your folks and tell them as openly, calmly, and honestly as you can about what's going on. Let them know you could use their advice on how to cope—the smallest suggestion might have a big impact.

Siblings and stepsiblings, especially the older and wiser types, can also be valuable resources for advice, especially when it comes to dealing with stresses in your social life or dealing with parents. Even if you don't have the closest relationship, your sibling might surprise you by being supportive in unexpected ways if he or she knows you're struggling with something.

What if your parents are responsible for much of your stress in the first place? Then there's even *more* reason to talk with them about what's going on—they just might not be aware that they're a source of angst. Bringing it to light may encourage them to make some helpful changes on their end. Again, to optimize your chances of success, approach your parents calmly and with respect—not in the heat of the moment—and your message will be more likely to get through the way you intend. Don't accuse—open a discussion, and be prepared to listen to what they have to say too.

FRIENDS

Leaning on close friends can be invaluable when you're at wits' end. Because friends often have unique, in-the-trenches insight into your plight, they can offer an insider's perspective like no one else.

What about when friendship complications are the source of your stress and angst? Hopefully, your friendship is solid enough to handle a little honest communication, and you can air your concerns directly to your friend. Learn more about handling friendship stresses on page 111.

MENTORS

World leaders have them. So do CEOs of Fortune 500 companies, famous actors, and professional athletes. So why shouldn't you? Mentors are those people who advise us, guide us, and steer us in the right direction when it comes to

schoolwork, relationships, future dreams . . . life. A mentor wants to see you succeed, and that means being there for you when you're in need of support.

You can lean on mentors to help you navigate the college application process, study for tests, review your job applications, give you career guidance . . . even help you figure out creative solutions to sticky social or family situations.

Don't know how to find one? Mentors can be just about anyone—an older student, a favorite teacher, a relative, a fellow volunteer. Some mentor relationships are informal—your mentor may not even know you consider her to be a role model or adviser. Other relationships are more structured—you may be paired up with your mentor through an official organization like Girls Inc. or your school.

To connect with a mentor through an organization near you, visit Mentoring.org (www.mentoring.org), a comprehensive website with a ton of information on all aspects of mentoring. Search by zip code for opportunities in your community.

TEACHERS AND COACHES

If you spend a lot of time involved in sports, school, and extracurriculars, you've probably already developed positive, supportive relationships with some of your teachers and coaches. These adults know you very well, and depending on the situation, turning to a teacher or coach for help might seem less threatening than going to your parents.

While teachers and coaches can be great sources of guidance, they may also be directly responsible for the stress you're experiencing. Because they want you to succeed, they sometimes respond by dumping on the pressure. If that's the case, go straight to the source in asking for help.

If you're convinced you can't make a deadline for a class or your coach is pushing you past your breaking point, talk to him or her. Ask for an extension on the assignment or to be excused from a practice and explain why. Even if you're convinced your request will be denied, what's the harm in asking? You might be pleasantly surprised with the outcome.

GUIDANCE COUNSELORS AND SCHOOL PSYCHOLOGISTS

Since so much stress is caused by ever-increasing academic pressure, guidance counselors and school psychologists are an ideal resource when it comes to things like figuring out what courses to take and when to take them, making sure your bases are covered regarding prerequisites, putting you in touch with alumni who can offer you insight into different colleges, helping you create a manageable schedule, and helping you put together a plan for reaching your goals. Many schools schedule periodic meetings between students and these on-site counselors, but in some larger schools, you may have to seek them out for yourself. They're there for *you*, so take advantage of them!

CLUBS AND ORGANIZATIONS

You may not think of turning to members of school clubs when you're in the midst of a stressful crisis. But by being a member of a special interest club (from photography to the Gay-Straight Alliance) or joining a team, you strengthen your core foundation by regularly surrounding yourself with people who share your interests and/or beliefs. When you spend time in a group where you're able to enjoy things you're passionate about or safely explore new ideas and interests, you're also creating a support network that may play a role in preventing stressful crises in the first place!

RELIGIOUS LEADERS AND YOUTH GROUPS

If you're involved in an organized religion or youth group, that might be a core component of your ongoing support system.

How to Ask for Help

We've covered the *when* and the *where* of asking for help. All that's left is the *how*. Luckily, asking for help is relatively painless. Here's how to get the support and help you need:

- **Admit that you need help.** Before you can ask, you've got to be straight with yourself and realize that reaching out for help is in your best interest.

- **Remember that asking for help is the smart thing to do.** Getting help from someone not only eases your load, but the input from others can also offer you new and inspired ways to approach your stressful situation.

- **If you know what you need, be specific in asking for it.** Often people want to help out, but they don't know what to do. Be clear about how people in your support system can best be there for you.

- **Learn to accept help when people offer it.** Many of us have been programmed to respond automatically to offers of help with, "No thanks, I've got it." It's time to retrain yourself—people don't typically offer support unless they're willing and able to give it. From now on, assume that offers of help are genuine!

- **Know that the helper gets something out of it too.** By accepting a friend's help, you're giving her the chance to feel good about the role she played. Who doesn't like to feel as though her contribution is appreciated?

- **Don't take it personally if the person you ask says no.** Sometimes those we turn to for help aren't able to step up to the plate for us. When that happens, remind yourself that they are exercising their right to speak their own truth (see chapter five) and don't make it mean anything other than they're too busy to help you this time.

Be the Help You Want

You don't have to wait until you're in crisis mode to build your circle of support. By surrounding yourself with positive people who share your interests and care about you, you're creating a supportive foundation you can lean on in good times and bad.

Remember, having a support circle goes both ways. It works best when everyone in it has his or her needs met. This means being there for your friends in the same way you'd want them to be there for you. The next time you notice that someone in your support system is going through a stressful situation, take the lead and make it clear you're there for your friend. For more on stresses and friendships, see page 111.

Making It Stick

It may seem out of character the first time you do it, but asking for help gets easier with practice. Here are some suggestions for making this positive stress-reducing approach a regular habit.

- **Begin accepting offers of help in no-stress situations.** If someone says, "Can I get the door for you?" answer "Yes!" If a friend offers to pick up a coffee for you on the way to school, graciously reply, "Thanks . . . that would be great!" By reprogramming your responses so it becomes normal to accept offers of help from others, you'll be more likely to call in the reinforcements when stress is getting the best of you.

- **Be a friend who helps others when they need it.** By being a part of someone else's support system, you're setting the standard for the kind of support you would like when the tables are turned.

- **Practice asking for help in your everyday life.** Ask your sis if she'll help you fold the laundry, or see if your mom would be up for quizzing you on your notes the night before your science test. As you ask for help, don't make excuses or apologies—just be straightforward and honest. For example, "Ruby, I've got a ton of homework to wrap up and I'm running out of time. Would you mind helping me fold the clothes in the dryer?" Or, "Mom, I would be grateful if you could take a half hour to drill me on my science notes. I've got a quiz tomorrow and I want to make sure I know my stuff."

JOURNAL IT:

- **Make a list of five people you can turn to for help.** For each person, write down what it is that makes him or her a crucial part of your support circle, and what kinds of problems you feel you could talk to him or her about.

- **Write about one area of your life that is causing you stress.** Spend a few minutes exploring the "if onlys" in your journal. *If only my teacher would give me an extra day for this assignment* or *If only I could find someone to switch my work shift with this weekend.* Then choose one of these "if onlys" and try to make it a reality by reaching out to your support system and asking for help.

Quiz

Do you know how to ask for help when you need it?

1. You just started your job at a card shop in the mall a few weeks ago, and you're on the schedule two nights per week. But this week is midterms, and you could really use any extra time you can find to study. You:

   a. *ask for a day off—the worst your boss can say is no, and if she says yes, it will totally have been worth it.*

   b. *show up at work, but sneak in some studying during slow times and ask to leave early.*

c. *decide it's not worth the risk of annoying your boss. You can't afford to lose your job, so your grades will just have to suffer this term.*

2. A friend has been leaning on you hard ever since her parents announced their big split. You want to be there for her, but you're spending so much time consoling your friend that you're starting to ignore your own needs. You:

   a. *talk to your sister, your mom, or a mentor about what's going on, and ask him or her for advice on how to be a supportive friend while taking care of yourself at the same time.*

   b. *try to separate yourself from the drama in your friend's life and pull back from the friendship until the crisis is over.*

   c. *can't imagine not being there for your friend, so you suck it up and allow her stress to pile right on top of your own until you're both ready to blow.*

3. The application deadline for your dream college is coming up. You'd love to have your mentor review your essay, but you know she's got a busy, pressure-filled job. You:

   a. *approach her honestly and say that, while you realize how hectic her schedule is, you'd be grateful if she could devote even a half hour to reviewing your essay.*

   b. *hint about the help you need the next time you talk, hoping she'll take the bait and volunteer.*

c. *are afraid of stressing her out more, so you decide not to bother her with your essay—she's got much more important things to worry about than your college application.*

4. You've been home for almost a week with the flu, and you were so sick you couldn't even work on your term paper from bed. Now you're stressed about meeting your deadline, especially because your teacher has never shown much compassion for his students. You:

a. *ask to meet with your teacher after school to explain your situation and request an appropriate extension, explaining that you have a plan for completing the assignment.*

b. *sacrifice other things to get the assignment done, like skipping other homework assignments, canceling your babysitting gig, and holing up inside your house for a week.*

c. *are too intimidated to ask your teacher for an extension. You know he hasn't responded positively to other students in similar situations and you don't want to risk getting on his bad side.*

5. You've always been able to juggle it all effortlessly, but with the addition of your new role coordinating the homecoming pep rally, you suddenly realize that you've taken on too much. You:

a. *go to your close group of friends and ask them to help out, giving each one a specific task to ensure that everything for the rally goes off without a hitch.*

b. *decide to give yourself a break and not be as ambitious about accomplishing everything you wanted to for the rally. All you really need are some posters and a microphone, right?*

c. *tough it out and try to do it all yourself—if you can make it through the next two weeks without a breakdown, you can do just about anything.*

How'd you do? Add up your score and find out. Give yourself 0 points for every A, 10 points for every B, and 20 points for every C.

0–20 points: You know when you need help, and you know exactly how to ask for it, especially when it comes to handling your stress.

30–60 points: You take a more passive approach and like to give things a chance to work out before reaching out.

70–100 points: You tend to deny you need help and avoid asking for it, even when you know in your heart it might be the best thing to do.

CREATE AN AFFIRMATION ABOUT ASKING FOR AND ACCEPTING HELP

Write it down on an index card or piece of paper and tape it where you'll see it often. Here are a few examples:

- *My call for help is answered by the right person, at the right time, and in the right way.*

- *I am surrounded by supportive people who want to see me happy, balanced, and peaceful.*

- *By asking for help, I am doing something loving for myself.*

WHAT ANASTASIA DOES

"My boxer forces me to take a nice, long one-hour break every day. I leave my phone at home and just focus on the walk, letting my mind wander and daydream." —Anastasia Goodstein, SVP, The Ad Council, and author of Totally Wired: What Teens & Tweens Are Really Doing Online

GET INSPIRED

Rent the movie *Freedom Writers* or read the book it was based on, *The Freedom Writers Diary,* for a compelling true story about a group of high school students who created a powerful circle of support.

Dear Debbie,

My parents are always telling me to do better, that I can be better and that I can do greater things. How do I get them to back off, because I already work really hard?

Emma, age 16

Dear Emma,

Pressure from the parental units seems to be a common problem. I get lots of letters like yours from teens who are tired of feeling like nothing they do is good enough for their parents. No matter what your relationship with your folks is like, you owe it to all three of you to let them know what's going on. Your parents may acknowledge that they're pressuring you, but they might not realize that it is having very real, stressful side effects. Before you talk with your parents, think about the kind of help you'd like from them (beyond just having them back off). If you can give your parents a list of things they could do to help you succeed (such as give you gentle reminders about important dates, help you find a tutor for a class you're struggling with, or notice something once a day that you're doing really well), they may not feel the need to get on your case about things that cause you more angst. Good luck!

XOXO Debbie

TIME-OUT:
THE FRIENDSHIP SURVIVAL GUIDE

Your friends are a huge factor in your life. They're the people you lean on when you're upset, they help you remember not to take yourself so seriously, they have your back when you're in a tough spot, and they're a major source of fun! But such close relationships are bound to have their share of challenges. In fact, nearly 100 percent of girls polled for this book said that trouble with friends is a top source of stress.

Friendship Problems

I could fill a book about the complexities and stresses in friendships, but here are some basic survival tips for staying sane in the midst of common friendship dilemmas.

FRIENDSHIP FIGHTS

Considering how much time you spend with your friends, it's no surprise that just about every friendship goes through occasional conflicts. Friendship fights can get ugly in a hurry, especially when one or both parties tries to get others to take sides, or plays dirty by completely ignoring the person they're fighting with.

Though friendship fights will undoubtedly cause you stress, here are some ways to keep things in perspective and make your conflicts, and resolutions, as painless as possible:

- **Don't get others involved.** When a disagreement between two people turns into a group fight, sorting things out can be one huge mess. While you need to be able to share your feelings with your other friends, there's a big difference between doing that and trying to convince others to take your side.

- **Don't get sucked in to other fights.** Likewise, when you're not involved in a situation between two friends, don't contribute and make it *your* fight by choosing sides. You can be a sounding board without putting in your two cents.

- **Take a step back.** When you're in the midst of a friendship clash, the emotions can be intense. Give yourself space and alone time to reflect on the situation and your role in it and figure out what you hope the outcome will be.

- **Be patient.** While tiffs between friends can be over in a matter of hours, more serious fights can take days, weeks, and even months to resolve. If you're feeling especially hurt about something that happened in a friendship, take the time to get over it and get distance from the situation. By jumping back into a friendship before you've gotten over the hurt, you're bound to face the same challenges again down the road. Likewise, if you're over it but your friend isn't, be patient and give her the time to fully recover.

- **Write about what's going on.** Friendship challenges can leave you confused, insecure, and shell-shocked. Treat your journal like your new best friend and write down every last hurt feeling about the crisis. Getting it down on paper will be a source of emotional release, and it may also help you work out a creative solution to repairing your relationship.

LOVE AND CRUSHES

When you or your BFF has a serious thing for someone else, your friendship may be a casualty. Who hasn't gotten blown off by a friend when her new love interest suddenly took center stage? The rule of friendships may be "friends first, significant others second," but that's not always the way things go down. Here are some suggestions for dealing with matters of the heart:

- **Two-month rule.** Be forgiving of a friend who puts her new beau before you in the first two months of a new relationship, and ask her to give you the same leeway when the situation is reversed. But once that "honeymoon period" is over, make sure to put your friendship and relationship ratio back into balance.

- **No last-minute ditches.** Make a pact among your friends that no matter what's going on with a flame, you won't pull a last-minute change of plans and leave a friend in the lurch.

- **Make dates with your friend.** Significant others aren't the only ones who need to go on dates. Make sure to set aside time for just you and your friend (no boyfriends or girlfriends allowed) to hang out and do the things that are special to the two of you.

Friends in Need

When a close friend goes through a difficult time, it can be hard on you, too. You probably want to support her, but it's not always easy to know exactly what to do. No matter what the situation, here are some guidelines for being there for a friend:

- **Be there or be square.** This may seem obvious, but sometimes friends need to actually hear the words "I'm here for you if you need me" before opening up.

- **Listen well.** Listening is more than just saying "uh-huh" and nodding your head on cue. To be a good listener, focus on what your friend is saying, count to three before chiming in to make sure your friend has finished her thought, and have your talk face-to-face instead of over text message.

- **Don't judge.** When a friend shares her stressful situation with you, the last thing she wants is to feel judged or as if you don't approve. Try to keep your judgments, and unsolicited advice, to yourself, and instead focus on giving your friend what she needs in the moment. If she wants your advice, be honest *and* tactful.

- **Treat your friend.** A little distraction can be a great thing. If your friend is super stressed out, why not surprise her with a little gift or a getaway to the mall or the movies?

CREATING HEALTHY BOUNDARIES

When a friend goes through a difficult time, do you find your own mood sometimes shifts right along with hers? Do you become preoccupied with your friend's situation and try to ease her pain or come up with a solution? Do you feel like it's your job to make your friend feel better?

There's a big difference between being there for a friend and feeling responsible for your friend's happiness. But it can be challenging to draw healthy boundaries, especially if you've got a friend who's used to leaning on you in a crisis.

To create healthy boundaries in your friendships, follow these rules:

- Make sure you spend time with your friend where you talk about things other than her crises. If you notice that every time the two of you are together the conversation goes back to the same place, it's okay to ask her if you can have a break from talking about the challenge for a while.

- **Don't contribute to the drama.** Let your friend know that while you understand how upsetting her situation is, you know she is strong enough to get through it. Instead of using end-of-the-world language like "that's outrageous" or "how can you stand that?" use phrases like, "that's a tough situation" or "it sucks that you have to go through this right now."

- If you're taking on too much of your friend's stress to the point that it's starting to affect you, it's fine (and actually necessary) to take a step back from the situation. Be up front and honest with your friend, and explain that while you want to be there for her, you need a hiatus for your own well-being.

Knowing When to Draw the Line

When the dynamics of a friendship are creating more stress than good in your life, it might be time to evaluate the relationship and decide whether or not it's worth keeping around. Now, I'm not saying that friendships should be all sunshine and cupcakes 24/7. But they should be a source of positive energy—they have to bring something of value to your life, and you have to like the person you are when you're with that friend. Most important, you should feel like your friend will be there when you need her the most.

To find out if it's time to reevaluate a friendship, ask yourself these questions:

- Do I act differently or not like myself when I'm with this friend?

- Do I feel good about myself when I'm with this friend and after we've just spent time together?

- Am I getting something positive out of our relationship?

- Is there a trust bond between us?

- Do I ever feel like my friend is using or taking advantage of me?

- Would my friend be there for me if I reached out to her when I was in a jam?

- Does my friend show interest in listening to things that are important to me?

Depending on your answers, it may be time to make some changes. If you're unsure about what to do, try talking with the friend in question and share your concerns with her. She may be unaware of the imbalance and be more than willing to pick up the slack.

JOURNAL IT:

Sit down with a friend, write out these statements in your journals, and then swap with each other. Take your time completing the statements about your friendship, return your journals, and read each other's responses. You'll both gain some valuable insight into your relationship!

1. I'm lucky to have you as a friend because you are . . .

2. One of my favorite friendship memories with you is . . .

3. I'm happiest about our friendship when . . .

4. If there is one thing about me you'd be surprised to know, it would be . . .

5. You make me feel special when you . . .

6. One of your best qualities is . . .

7. Sometimes I get frustrated when you . . .

8. I value our friendship because . . .

9. When I'm feeling upset, the thing I need from you the most is . . .

10. When I think about our friendship twenty years from now, I imagine . . .

GETTING PERSPECTIVE

When you're completely overwhelmed with stress and your life's out of balance, it's easy to believe that things just couldn't get any worse. Sometimes the best way to keep stress from having so much control over your life is to take a giant step back and get a little perspective.

Many times, checking in with a friend and having him or her remind you that things really aren't that bad is all it takes. But if you're in need of a bigger kick in the reality butt, reflecting on your own past, comparing your stresses with what's happening outside of your immediate world, or putting yourself in someone else's shoes ought to do the trick.

GETTING PERSPECTIVE: Viewing your stress, and your life, in the context of the "big picture" in order to feel more at peace with your own stressful circumstances. Ideal for reducing stress related to:

- feeling like your problems are the "end of the world"

- being stressed out about the possibility of failure or inadequacy

- being concerned about not meeting people's expectations

- feeling insecure about fitting in

- feeling pressure to look and be a certain way

Perspective on Your Past

Have you ever been humiliated, embarrassed, caught in the middle of a family crisis, concerned over a loved one's illness, or felt like you just royally screwed up? Stroll down memory lane and no doubt you'll recall times when you were sure the end of the world as you knew it was imminent. Revisiting past crises and reflecting on the impact they do or don't have on you today can remind you of your ability to persevere even in the face of the most difficult challenges, or remind you that sometimes problems that seem like the biggest deal in the world end up not mattering at all the next week. Stressful situations that may have seemed insurmountable even a year ago have probably lost their impact. Hopefully, you can look back and ask yourself, *What was the big deal?*

The next time life dumps a new stressful situation in your lap, remember that you rose to the challenge in the past and feel secure in the knowledge that this time will be no different.

Try this experiment. Think about a memory from the recent past that caused you immense grief. This could be anything, from getting the flu the day of your first school dance or telling your BFF about your secret crush only to have her leak his identity to the entire school.

Got your memory? Good. Now close your eyes and ask yourself:

1. Did the situation eventually get resolved?

2. What was the long-term result of the situation?

3. Does the outcome still affect me today?

4. Did the situation end up being as bad as I initially thought?

5. Did I learn or gain anything valuable from the experience?

Hopefully you'll discover that, with the passing of time, things that once seemed unbearable usually turn out to be okay. I'm not saying you need to have fond memories of the situation or find humor in it—it may still be painful to think about. But the point is, *you survived*. Remind yourself that things causing you angst today will most likely seem "not so bad" down the road.

Maybe one of these stressful past events actually had a *positive* side effect . . . that whole idea that *everything happens for a reason*. Maybe you learned the hard way that you're stronger than you thought. Maybe you discovered that you're comfortable speaking up for yourself or that you have an incredibly supportive circle of friends, or you learned that someone you thought was a true friend really wasn't and realized you'd be healthier and happier without the stress of that person in your life. Lessons might be painful, but what you take away in knowledge about yourself is often well worth it.

Big-Picture Perspective

Need another technique for putting stress into perspective? Try looking at the big picture of any stressful situation. By "big picture," I'm talking about recognizing that you are just one being in an immense global society, or stepping back and seeing where your stressor fits in with the big scheme of things when it comes to difficulties in life.

While I was writing my book, *In Their Shoes*, I interviewed many women who work long hours in highly stressful jobs. When I asked one woman how she found balance in her life despite her busy schedule, she told me that when she starts taking her stress too seriously, she reminds herself that she's not performing open-heart surgery. You know . . . there's no heart in the cooler she's got to deliver to the operating room.

I laughed at the time, but when I reflected on our talk, I realized that her metaphor was spot-on. Most of our daily stressors don't involve life-and-death decisions. We're not making choices that could mean the difference between a meal on the table or no food for a week. Most of us don't worry about where we're going to sleep each night.

Now, I'm not saying that just because you're not facing life-and-death challenges, your issues aren't important or valid. No one should belittle anyone else's discomfort or stress. But I do think it's worth taking a step back, looking at what's going on in your life in relation to the big picture, and considering whether or not your challenge is as dire as you're building it up to be in your head.

Do you need an extra boost getting big-picture perspective? Here are some statistics about the lives of teens around the world to put your stresses into sharp focus:

- Having trouble with your boyfriend? Consider this: *Many teen girls around the world are forced into arranged marriages by the time they're fourteen or fifteen years old.*

- Sick of facing pressures at school? At least you have the option: *Millions of girls around the world are pulled out of school by the age of ten (or never go to school in the first place) to help out at home or to work.*

- Can't seem to get along with your parents? Consider this: *Millions of teens in the world have lost their parents to HIV/AIDS, and many are HIV-positive themselves.*

- Stressed about bullies on your school grounds? Many teens live with violence every moment of every day: *Teenagers across the globe are living in the midst of wars and civil unrest.*

Volunteering

It might seem odd to talk about volunteering in a book that aims to help you reduce stress and create balance. After all, why would I suggest getting involved in *yet another* activity? The reason is simple: Volunteering is an excellent way to get perspective in a jiffy and to do something for yourself *and* for others at the same time. By volunteering with an organization whose mission you believe in, you can (1) experience seeing things from a different point of view, (2) forget about your own problems for a while, and (3) step inside someone else's shoes for a reality check. Even a small commitment, like spending one afternoon a month helping out with an important cause, can equal big rewards. By volunteering, you can enjoy stress-relief benefits such as:

- gaining valuable experience while reducing your stress

- becoming inspired and motivated by the work you're doing

- feeling less hopeless about global stressors because you're actively doing something to make a difference

- fulfilling graduation requirements and adding meat to your college application while making a positive difference

- getting a lot of perspective in a short period of time

- connecting with your purpose, leading to a sense of balance in your life

You can find volunteer opportunities in just about any area of interest, to fit even the most limited schedule. Here are just a few ideas for different kinds of volunteer work that might inspire you, keep you balanced, and help reduce your stress all at the same time:

- Want to reconnect with the environment? Clean up garbage at a local park or beach.

- In need of some unconditional love? Walk or bathe dogs at a local animal shelter.

- Have a lot to share? Tutor underprivileged kids through an after-school program.

- Want to get your hands dirty? Help set up a community garden.

- Need some instant big-picture perspective? Serve meals at a homeless shelter.

To learn about volunteer opportunities available near you, visit www.volunteermatch.org and search by zip code.

Being Thankful

"Being thankful" is a simple concept. But don't mistake simple for inconsequential. There is a growing body of scientific research that speaks to the very real side-effects of regularly practicing gratitude, including having things like a boosted immune system, lower blood pressure, higher levels of positive emotions like joy and happiness, and less feelings of loneliness and isolation. As a perspective shifter, being thankful, or celebrating something or someone in your life that brings you joy, comfort, or safety, can:

- shift your focus away from the negative aspects of a situation and toward the positive

- remind yourself that there is good in your life no matter how bad things get

- have a positive impact on your emotions and mental state of mind

Maybe you're thankful for your family, your dog, your down comforter. Maybe you're thankful for your health, your sense of humor, your friends. The point is, we all have good things in our lives. Feeling gratitude about even the smallest thing can have an immediate impact on your state of mind. And hey, it's way better than complaining.

Creating a gratitude practice is super simple. Just find a small notebook—a mini spiral-bound book from the drugstore works just fine—and leave it on your bedside table. Then, every night before you go to sleep, flip open to a blank page, write the date on the top, and jot down at least one thing you are grateful for that day. Some days you might have a dozen things pop into your head and other days you may have to really reach to find even one tiny thing. Commit to keeping your gratitude journal for at least thirty days and see how it changes your attitude.

Making It Stick

Putting things into perspective takes practice, since your first instinct when you're stressed out probably isn't to pause and reflect. Here are some suggestions for making this healthy habit stick:

- **Make a regular commitment to volunteering,** even if it's only a once-a-year thing. By scheduling the volunteer opportunity ahead of time, you build some foolproof perspective-getting time into your life.

- **Tell a close friend your plan for keeping things in perspective.** Give him or her instructions to say the following to you the next time you complain about the stresses you're under: "Remember . . . you're not doing open-heart surgery!"

- **Don't forget to laugh!** Surrounding yourself with friends who make you laugh will keep you from taking every little stressful thing too seriously. If your friends aren't funny, live-stream some of your favorite comedies, microwave some popcorn, and sit down for a healthy, rib-splitting release.

JOURNAL IT:

- **Write down five stressful events or situations from your past,** and explore how those situations impact you today. Are you still stressed about them? Did you learn anything from those experiences?

- **Ask your mom and dad to tell you about a time when they were particularly stressed out as teenagers.** After you hear their stories, write about them in your journal, and think about how you would have handled the same situations if you were in their shoes.

- **Take the Grateful Challenge.** For the next month, try being thankful—truly *acknowledging* and *feeling* the gratitude—for one thing every day.

Quiz

How much perspective do you have when it comes to stressful situations? To find out, circle what your typical response to these scenarios would be.

1. Your favorite jeans are in the wash the night of a big party.

- *Big-time emergency (5 points)*

- *No biggie (0 points)*

2. You open your backpack to get down to studying, only to realize you grabbed the wrong textbook when you left school.

   - *Big-time emergency (5 points)*

   - *No biggie (0 points)*

3. Your crush hasn't replied to your comment on his Instagram pic and you know he's been online.

   - *Big-time emergency (5 points)*

   - *No biggie (0 points)*

4. Your parents' car broke down (again) and you have to find a ride home from cross-country practice.

   - *Big-time emergency (5 points)*

   - *No biggie (0 points)*

5. The application to your dream college is due in two days and you've decided to rewrite your essay from scratch.

   - *Big-time emergency (5 points)*

   - *No biggie (0 points)*

6. You've got a migraine headache the day of the SATs.

   - *Big-time emergency (5 points)*

   - *No biggie (0 points)*

7. Tonight's the biggest pool party of the summer and you just got your period.

   - *Big-time emergency (5 points)*

   - *No biggie (0 points)*

8. A storm has knocked out power at your house so you can't watch the live season finale of your favorite show.

   - *Big-time emergency (5 points)*

   - *No biggie (0 points)*

9. Your BFF just admitted that she's got a thing for your crush.

   - *Big-time emergency (5 points)*

   - *No biggie (0 points)*

10. You fill out your calendar and realize that four of your classes have midterms on the exact same day.

    - *Big-time emergency (5 points)*

    - *No biggie (0 points)*

SCORING

How'd you do? If you scored more than twenty points, then your perspective may be a bit out of whack. While I certainly understand that missing out on a big season finale could be considered seriously stressful, in the big picture it's not that big a deal. Try taking a step back the next time you're feeling stressed and see if you can put your crisis into better perspective.

CREATE AN AFFIRMATION THAT HELPS YOU KEEP PERSPECTIVE

Write it down on an index card or piece of paper and tape it up where you'll see it often. Here are a few examples:

- *I am thankful for the many blessings in my life.*

- *I learn and grow from every experience, no matter how challenging.*

- *By being aware of the plight of others, I appreciate my own circumstances for what they are.*

Got a stressed-out friend? Here are some tips for helping her chill out:

- *Surprise her with an escape date—go to the movies, go to the mall, take the bus downtown and check out the art museum.*

- *Plan a sleepover and stay up all night watching your favorite movies.*

- *Make her a mini-scrapbook of happy memories the two of you share.*

- *Remind your friend of a stressful situation from the past that turned out to be not so bad.*

- *Unless your friend is a surgical resident, jokingly remind her that she's not performing open-heart surgery!*

GET INSPIRED

The classic John Hughes film *The Breakfast Club* is worth watching to see how a diverse group of high school students gets some perspective while serving a daylong detention. Plus, you'll have a good laugh!

Dear Debbie,

I'm always stressed out about relationships. I'm constantly worried about whether or not the boy I like likes me back or if I'm too ugly for him to like me . . . stuff like that. How can I stop stressing about this?

Dehlia, age 13

Dear Dehlia,

Relationships can definitely be the source of a ton of stress, especially when you're not sure where you stand with the guy you like. The feelings can be very intense, and when you're focused on relationship angst, sometimes nothing else seems to matter. You might want to try putting your crush stress into perspective before it takes over your life. One way to do this is by flipping through your yearbook and pointing out all the other boys you've crushed on in the past year or two. Remember how strongly you felt about them at the time? Did the feelings fade away? Did your crush turn out to be who or what you expected him to be? If the boy you're currently into works out, great. If not, know things haven't always worked out the way you wanted in the past and you survived, so you will this time too. With that attitude, you'll spend less time stressing about your guy and he'll have a better chance to experience the real you! Good luck!

XOXO Debbie

WHAT ALICE DOES

*"When I trust that everything happens the way it's supposed
to, then I stop putting so much pressure on myself. I reflect
on the past and know that I have many examples in my life of
things working out as they are meant to be. Even when what has
happened in the past has not been something that I was happy
about, it still taught me what I needed to know at the time."*

—Dr. Alice Wilder, Educational Psychologist

WHAT JENNA DOES

*"I find a way to take the focus off myself and move my gaze
outward—go for a walk, look at some trees, take a breath,
exercise. Hell, just read the headlines and you'll be grateful for
the problems you have."*

—Jenna Stern, Actor

TIME-OUT:
MORE THAN STRESS? WHEN IT'S TIME TO GET PROFESSIONAL HELP

While stress is a normal part of life for everyone, it can also be a symptom of something more serious going on. If that's the case, it's time to get professional help. If you're experiencing any or all of the problems described below, you need to widen your support circle and get the outside help of people who are trained in dealing with your issue.

Maybe you think you can handle the problem all on your own or that you're just going through a phase. Maybe the idea of "professional help" sounds too intense for you. Well, know that help comes in many different forms. You don't need to go to some fancy rehab center to get help—you can call an anonymous hotline or ask your doctor for a referral to a counselor, or even see if your school has a psychologist on staff who could point you in the right direction. The truth is, some problems are too big to face alone. Read on and see if you fall into any of these categories, and then find a resource listed below to get help today.

The Issue: Depression and Feeling Suicidal

There's a difference between feeling down or stressed and being depressed. People who are depressed say they feel as though there's a dark cloud hanging over them. No matter what's happening in their life (good and bad), people who are depressed feel sad and hopeless much of the time. And while some of the symptoms of depression, such as insomnia and a loss of appetite, are similar to those for stress, depression doesn't go away when the stress ends. What's worse, if untreated, depression may lead to suicidal thoughts or attempted suicide.

THE TREATMENT

Depression can take a while to recover from, and the most successful cure is therapy, medication, or a combination of the two.

GET HELP

Find out more about depression, suicide prevention, and where to get help through these websites and hotlines:

- iFred, the International Foundation for Research and Education on Depression (www.ifred.org)
- Girls and Boys Town 24-Hour National Hotline (1-800-448-3000) or www.girlsandboystown.org
- National Suicide Prevention Lifeline (1-800-273-TALK)
- Samariteens Suicide Prevention Hotline (1-800-252-TEEN)
- Hopeline (1-800-442-HOPE)

The Issue: Eating Disorders

Statistics show that most teenage girls diet at some point, or at the very least, struggle with body image issues. But when does wanting to drop a few pounds or feeling insecure about one's body cross the line and become an eating disorder?

True eating disorders, such as bulimia (bingeing and purging) and anorexia (excessive dieting and starvation), are considered to be psychological illnesses. And while people who suffer from these disorders come in all shapes, sizes, and ages, many share some commonalities, such as having low self-esteem, having trouble at home, being anxious, being the victim of bullying or abuse, or having difficulty expressing their emotions.

Whatever the cause, eating disorders can be extremely challenging to cure. While someone with a drinking problem can avoid alcohol, people with eating disorders can't avoid eating . . . they have to find a way to come to terms with their illness and change their relationship with food.

THE TREATMENT

The most successful forms of treatment for eating disorders involve therapy or counseling, often involving the whole family.

GET HELP

To find out more about eating disorders or to talk with someone about your concerns right now, take advantage of these resources:

- National Eating Disorders Association (www.nationaleatingdisorders.org)
- Bulimia and Self-Help 24-Hour Hotline (314-588-1683)

The Issue: Self-Mutilation

Studies show that one in two hundred teen girls regularly cuts or self-mutilates. Many girls say they cut, pick, rub, or even burn themselves because it helps them release their pain, emotions, stress, and anxiety. They're often girls whose lives look perfect on the outside—they get good grades, come from good families, and are active and popular in school—but inside they're full of turmoil.

Because cutters tend to make small cuts that heal, many don't think it's a big deal or that it has any serious ramifications. But that couldn't be further from the truth. Besides the fact that cutting, picking, and burning can leave permanent physical and emotional scars, some self-mutilators escalate their behavior to abuse drugs and alcohol, or may eventually attempt suicide.

THE TREATMENT

The best treatment for self-mutilation is therapy or counseling, where you can work with a specialist to discover the reasons why you cut and come up with methods to cope with those issues in a healthy and safe way.

GET HELP

You'll find a lot of information on how and where to get help at S.A.F.E. Alternatives (Self-Abuse Finally Ends): www.selfinjury.com (1-800-DONTCUT).

LOOKING
IN

8

DIY THERAPY

Imagine what would happen if you didn't pass your history final. Or if your parents announced that you would be moving and starting at a new school in the fall. Or how would you feel if your group of friends suddenly turned on one another in a social version of World War III? Would it be the *end of the world* for you?

It doesn't have to be.

About ten years ago, when I was going through my own seriously stressful "end-of-the-world" sequence of events, I decided to do something completely new—I went to therapy. This wasn't lie-on-the-couch, pour-your-heart-out, analyze-every-painful-event-since-birth therapy. It was a form of cognitive therapy called REBT, which stands for rational emotive behavioral therapy.

Now, I'm not a therapist, but I did learn *a lot* about behavioral therapy during my years visiting the Albert Ellis Institute in New York City. And I still use the tools I learned back then to get through the daily stresses and struggles of life. Once you understand the principles behind it, you can apply them to just about anything that's happening. With a little practice, stopping your stress-related emotions from spiraling out of control might even become second nature.

COGNITIVE BEHAVIORAL THERAPY: The idea that changing the way you think will change the way you feel. Ideal for reducing stress related to:

- feeling as though things are always out of your control

- struggling with overwhelming emotions

- facing problems within your family or circle of friends

- feeling pressure to meet the unrealistic expectations of yourself or those around you

- struggling with peer pressure to look, be, and act a certain way

DIY Therapy 101

Cognitive behavioral therapies like REBT are based on the idea that our *emotions* are controlled by our *thoughts*. So if we can change our negative thoughts, then we can change the negative emotions that go along with them.

What does this have to do with stress? Well, if you're experiencing the emotional turmoil of stress, then you may be telling yourself something irrational that's making you feel bad. If you can change what you're telling yourself and replace it with healthier and more rational thoughts, then you can stop your emotional spiral (or at least slow it down considerably).

Say you're a sophomore in high school and you just found out you didn't make the varsity soccer team, something you were absolutely counting on. If you tell yourself that not making the varsity team means you're worthless or that your chances at a soccer scholarship someday are over, chances are you're going to feel the emotions that go along with those thoughts—despair, devastation, distress.

But if you can *change the thought* and realize that sealing your fate over one coach's opinion of your soccer skills doesn't make a lot of sense, then your emotions don't have to be so extreme. Sure, you might still be bummed out and disappointed, but you can *deal*.

How to Benefit from DIY Therapy

Cognitive behavioral therapy can easily be applied to almost any situation that creates angst in your life. Here is a simple, three-step approach for confronting those out-of-control, stressful emotions and creating a state of mind you can deal with:

Step 1: Identify the emotions

Step 2: Identify the thoughts behind the emotions

Step 3: Dispute the thoughts and get rational

HERE'S AN EXAMPLE OF HOW IT WORKS

Say your ninth-grade English teacher, Mr. X, decides to read your *very* personal essay out loud in class. As if this weren't bad enough, you realize he chose your paper so he could rip it to shreds in the process, leaving you humiliated and in tears. Everyone, and I mean *everyone*, turns and stares. Realizing that maybe he's gone too far, your teacher tries to make light of the situation by cracking a bad joke, which only makes things worse. You close your eyes and will yourself to disappear, but when this fails, you're forced to suck it up for another ten minutes, red-faced and shell-shocked, before the bell rings. You're in a bad emotional place, to say the least, and you're not sure you'll recover from this meltdown.

Step 1: Identifying the Emotions

Crying in front of the whole class? Yikes . . . what were you thinking? Chances are you're feeling some, if not all, of these emotions:

- humiliation
- embarrassment
- despair
- anger
- rage

But what good do any of these emotions actually do you? Anger and rage just fester and eventually fill your head with helpless thoughts of revenge. Couple that with the other emotions, and you're well on your way to a downward emotional spiral. Considering you've got a big audition for the musical after school, the timing for this self-esteem plummet couldn't be worse.

Step 2: Identifying the Thoughts Behind the Emotions

If you're feeling any of the above emotions, my guess is you're placing some pretty harsh judgments on yourself. Do any of these thoughts sound about right?

- I should have told the teacher off and walked out of class.
- I shouldn't have cried in front of everyone.
- I'm a crybaby.
- No one will ever look at me the same.
- Any chance of dating [insert name here] is over.
- Mr. X is a horrible, hateful person, and he shouldn't have humiliated me like that!

Who can blame you for thinking those things? But you don't have to go down that road. There's another way to look at the situation.

Step 3: Disputing the Thoughts and Getting Rational

It's time to go through each of the above thoughts and question them one by one. Since you're feeling so bad because of your irrational thoughts, it only makes sense that challenging and reframing them will have a positive effect on your emotions.

Thoughts: *I should have told the teacher off and walked out of class* and *I shouldn't have cried in front of everyone.* **Reality:** You can't change what's already happened. Placing judgment on yourself and what you "should have" done doesn't do any good. Besides, what's wrong with crying in that situation? Your paper was very personal, and the teacher didn't treat you with respect. Any reasonable person would have been upset by what happened. And telling the teacher off? That might have felt good in the moment but probably would have resulted in a *much worse* situation than the one you're in now.

Thought: *I'm a crybaby.* **Reality:** Who says crying makes you a baby? Everybody cries . . . even the hottest guy in class gets choked up by the occasional chick flick or baseball game. It's part of being a thinking, feeling human being. Hey, you should be glad that you're in touch with your emotions and aren't repressing them—you're lessening the chances of a major blowup down the road!

Thought: *No one will ever look at me the same.* **Reality:** Yeah, so maybe they won't. But the truth is, you can't control how anyone else *feels* about you, let alone *looks* at you, so dwelling on this one is a no-win situation. Besides, what if people *do* look at you differently? Maybe they'll respect your ability to express yourself. Maybe they'll empathize with you for being put on the spot by such a jerky teacher.

Thought: *Any chance of dating* [insert name here] *is over.* **Reality:** The cliché sound bite here, of course, is "If someone doesn't like you for who you are, then that person's not worth having around." But clichés are often based in reality. If [*insert name here*] isn't interested in you because you reacted honestly, imagine what he or she would be like if you were dating. No thanks!

Thought: *Mr. X is a horrible, hateful person, and he shouldn't have humiliated me like that!* **Reality:** I don't know if Mr. X is truly hateful and horrible, but he certainly acted insensitively. But since you can't control what other people do, saying he shouldn't have done it is a waste of time—you can only control how *you* feel about it. *Let it go!*

Once you've challenged those irrational thoughts, you'll be surprised to see that your new, rational thinking leads to feeling new, healthier emotions:

Old Emotion	New Emotion
humiliation and embarrassment	disappointment
despair	displeasure
anger and rage	annoyance

And voilà. Emotional spiral *stopped.* End-of-the-world dramas that may have pushed you over the edge at one time no longer hold their evil grasp over you.

When you're feeling a lot of stress, it's easy to place the blame for how you're feeling on the outside world. You might blame your stress and its accompanying emotions on impossible deadlines, the ridiculous demands placed on you, a lack of understanding among your friends and family, and the many things in your life that are simply outside your control.

While it's good to recognize the sources of your stress, when you excuse the way you're feeling by placing the full blame on outside influences, you give away your power to improve the situation. Even if external challenges are the *source* of your stress, it's the *way you choose to perceive* those challenges that determines how you respond to them.

As Dr. Jay Winner, author of *Stress Management Made Simple*, writes, "The present moment can only be the way it is. Much of our stress comes from wishing it were different."

AWFULIZING

I don't think you'll find the word "awfulizing" in the dictionary, but it's a term my therapist taught me to describe what many of us do when we're feeling overwhelmed or upset about something. We tend to use all kinds of "worst-case scenario" language, like:

- It's *awful.*
- It's *terrible.*
- I *can't stand it.*
- It's going to *kill me.*

- It's an *impossible* situation.

- It's the *worst thing* ever.

If those are the kinds of words you use to describe a stressful situation, then of course the way you're feeling will rise to the occasion. A subtle change in the words you use can make a huge difference in the way you feel. What if you rewrote the above phrases using more "rational" terms?

- It's *awful.* → It's a *bummer.*

- It's *terrible.* → It's *unfortunate.*

- *I can't stand it.* → I *wish* I didn't have to go through this.

- It's going to *kill* me. → This *isn't how I'd prefer* things to go.

- It's an *impossible* situation. → It's a *setback.*

- It's the *worst thing* ever. → It's a *disappointment.*

Now, I know you're not going to walk around saying things like, "Wow, this isn't how I'd prefer this situation to have happened," but you get the point. By making your language less desperate and dark, your emotional responses will follow suit. From now on, something doesn't have to be "the end of the world." It can just be a setback, a bummer, a pain in the butt. You know that you *can* stand it and you *can* get through anything.

Sometimes the best antidote to "awfulizing" is to go ahead and imagine the worst-case scenario for your stressful situation. For example, say you're stressed out about not getting into your dream college, and you're dwelling on how your world will be over if you don't get in. Well, go ahead and imagine you don't get in and think about what you would do then. Would you go to your second-choice school? Take classes at a community college, ace them, and reapply next year? Usually, our worst-case scenario ends up not being as terrible as we might imagine. Once you realize what rock bottom is, you can take the fear of the unknown out of the equation and ultimately get rid of your angst.

THE BIG CHOICE

Perhaps the most stressful thing about daily life is that so much of it is completely beyond our control. We can't control how others will feel, think, or behave. We can't control what happens in the world when it comes to the job market, the economy, or the environment.

I used to "what if" things to death, wasting tons of time and energy worrying about things I couldn't change. *What if I don't get into my number one college? What if I never fall in love? What if I can't find the right job? What if I don't qualify for districts in track?* Then one day I realized that whether I worried or not, the outcome was going to be the same. That's an important thought, so let me say it again: Whether you worry or not, the outcome is the same. Your worrying won't make one bit of difference when it comes to how things are going to pan out other than to cause you unnecessary stress and emotional burnout. In fact, dwelling on the bad things that could happen may make them more likely to come to pass.

The choice is yours. Are you going to waste all of that energy being worried and stressed out, or are you going to let go of that useless emotion and focus on doing the best you can to move forward?

Here's another non-word word my therapist turned me on to: "shoulding." Shoulding is when you use the word "should" to describe things that you or someone else did, the idea being that better choices could have been made. For example:

- I *should have* realized that was going to happen.
- I *should have* studied more for the test.
- I *shouldn't have* trusted her with my secret.
- She *shouldn't have* dissed me like that.

Using the word "should" is all about regret, something that can't be changed, or something that is completely out of your control. While there's value in reflecting on or analyzing what happened in order to learn or grow from the experience, spending time and energy being upset about things you can't change is just one huge waste. So try eliminating the word "should" from your vocabulary. You might find it gives you back your power when you're frustrated and stressed out about what might have been.

WHAT YOU THINK IS WHAT YOU ARE

It really all comes down to this—what we choose to think about becomes our reality. If we spend our timing thinking about how difficult something is or focusing on all the things happening in our world that are stressful and sucky, our world is going to continue to feel difficult, stressful, and sucky, plain and simple.

But when we choose to change our thoughts to ones that are less dramatic and more optimistic, and spend more time thinking about the good things in our life, peace and happiness will become a regular part of our day-to-day existence.

Making It Stick

Are you up to the challenge of replacing your irrational thoughts with rational ones as a way to reduce stress? Then here are some tips for putting this do-it-yourself therapy into practice:

- **Make a pact with a friend to lose the "negative-speak"** or not say things like "it's awful" or "I can't stand it" in your day-to-day conversations. Then gently remind each other to replace such negative-speak with more appropriate language, like "that really stinks" or "it sucks that I have to go through this."

- **Tune in to your emotions.** If you're feeling especially emotional, there's a good chance that an irrational thought (or several) is behind your feelings. When you sense you're being irrational, try using the three-step process outlined previously to challenge those thoughts and see how your emotions change.

JOURNAL IT:

- **Write down five to ten phrases or words** that you commonly use to describe a situation or scenario that is especially stressful. Would you consider any of the phrases to be "awfulizing" language? If so, brainstorm alternative phrases you could use instead, so the next time you find yourself in a similar situation, you can use less "dark and desperate" language.

- **Copy the DIY therapy steps below into your journal** or type it up on your computer and print out copies. Whenever you're faced with a situation that triggers an irrational emotional reaction, fill out this worksheet and get a grip.

- **Write about how you used the three-step process to stop an emotional spiral.** Having successful experiences to look back on will reinforce the strength of this technique.

DIY THERAPY BREAKDOWN

Step 1: Describe the event. (What is the situation or event that triggered your overly emotional or irrational response?)

Step 2: Identify the emotions. (What are you feeling right now in response to the event you described in Step 1? Be as honest as you can and describe as many emotions as possible.)

Step 3: Identify the thoughts. (What are you telling yourself that is making you experience the emotions you described in Step 2? NOTE: This step can be the hardest one . . . dig deep and think about what is at the core of your irrational thoughts that could be fueling this reaction.)

Step 4: Dispute the thoughts. (Go through each thought you described in Step 3 and dispute them one by one. As you challenge these thoughts, tap into the strength inside you to overcome these obstacles.)

Is it your natural instinct to "awfulize" when things don't go as you planned? Take the quiz to find out:

1. You're lying in bed one night when you suddenly realize you skipped the last question on your essay test in English Lit earlier that day. You consider it:

   a. *an inconvenience*

   b. *a total bummer*

   c. *the end of the world*

2. Your mom is sick, so you'll have to skip jazz band practice to take care of your brother after school. This is:

   a. *an inconvenience*

   b. *a total bummer*

   c. *the end of the world*

3. You just found out that the posters you designed for the career fair were printed on the wrong paper and in the wrong color. To you, this is:

   a. *an inconvenience*

   b. *a total bummer*

   c. *the end of the world*

4. When a cheating scandal comes to light, your physics teacher decides to disregard the last test—the same one you busted your butt to study for and earned a 98 percent on. You consider this:

   a. *an inconvenience*

   b. *a total bummer*

   c. *the end of the world*

5. You have an interview scheduled for an after-school job, but you are sick with laryngitis and can barely speak. This is:

   a. *an inconvenience*

   b. *a total bummer*

   c. *the end of the world*

SCORING

Mostly As: Great job . . . you know that getting all worked up over something that's out of your control won't make the situation any better.

Mostly Bs: Setbacks may throw you off track, but you can usually turn your thoughts around.

Mostly Cs: You tend to "awfulize" when things don't go the way you expect. Try replacing your "end of the world" thoughts with more rational ones.

CREATE A DO-IT-YOURSELF THERAPY AFFIRMATION

Write your affirmation on an index card or piece of paper and post it where you'll see it often. Use one of the examples below or create an affirmation of your own.

- *There is nothing life can throw at me that I cannot handle.*

- *I choose the way I feel, and I can choose to see the positive side of any situation.*

- *I don't waste energy worrying about things that are beyond my control.*

WHAT AMANDA DOES

"When I am feeling stress, I first focus on my breathing. I concentrate on breathing deeply in and out, which helps me to feel calm. Next I look at the situation and what is causing me to feel stress. I usually find it is one small piece, and not the entire situation."

—Amanda Koster, Photographer

Dear Debbie,

I'm going eighteen hours away from my family and friends for
university. I have one friend coming with me, which makes it
easier, but my other friend who was also supposed to come
has given in to her parents' wishes to stay close to home,
and now she won't let my other friend and me talk about
school in front of her. On top of that, I'm a little freaked out about going—I'm
leaving my whole life behind, I'm stressed about trying to get scholarships,
tuition payments, plan my courses, and finish up my courses in high school.
Sometimes I just want to give up, crawl into bed, and not wake up until
everything's been handled for me. How can I deal with all of this?

Risa, age 18

Dear Risa,

Going to college is a HUGE deal. It can be a scary transition, especially when you're going far away from home, and there's so much to arrange before you even get there. It sounds like you're feeling overwhelmed about all the unknowns and the decisions that lie ahead. With regard to your friend who is staying behind, don't stop being yourself around her or let resentment build up because she doesn't want to hear about your plans. At the end of the day, you can't control how your friend is feeling about the situation. The best thing you can do is be honest with her about what's going on, understand and respect where she's coming from, and give her the chance to be your friend in the way she knows how. With regard to the stresses relating to all your pre-college planning details, it sounds like you're telling yourself that you just can't get everything done . . . that it's too much . . . that it's too overwhelming. Why not try using rational language and see how it affects how you're feeling? For example, instead of thinking you *can't* get everything done, why not tell yourself that it's going to be *challenging* to get everything done. Instead of saying that it's just *too overwhelming*, why not tell yourself that while *it's a lot to do*, millions of new college students do it every year and survive. Lastly, don't forget to enjoy this exciting time in your life. Sometimes the scariest leaps are the ones that yield the most rewards. Good luck with school!

XOXO Debbie

9

JOURNALING

I'll never forget the year I got my first diary. It was my eighth birthday. I'd had a Halloween-themed birthday party (I dressed up as a panda bear), and my friend Gretchen presented me with a Holly Hobbie diary (yes, this was a *long time ago*), and I was thoroughly entranced by the whole thing, especially the idea of a lock and the accompanying key that promised the writing inside would be for my eyes only. And so began my love affair with journaling—writing about my intimate thoughts and ideas as a way to express myself and unload everything going on in my head.

Millions of people keep journals—maybe you're one of them. And if you are, then you probably already know that writing in a journal can be an excellent way to download, relieve stress, and discover a little peace in your life. No judgments, no limitations, no expectations . . . what happens in your journal is between you and you.

JOURNALING: Regularly writing your thoughts and ideas in a journal or diary. Ideal for reducing stress related to:

- going through an identity crisis

- feeling like no one understands you

- being confused about how to handle a challenging social situation

- having pent-up stress

- dealing with family problems

- exploring your dreams for the future

- worrying about illness or the death of a friend or family member

What Is a Journal?

There are endless options for the means and methods you can use to download your thoughts. What feels like the best fit for you?

- **Traditional journal or blank book:** You can find these at any bookstore; they come in lined or unlined paper and in a ton of different formats, from leather-bound to those with plastic, board, or cloth covers.

- **Blog:** You can set up a blog for free using a platform like Wordpress, Blogger, or Tumblr, or create a blog on other social networking sites.

- **Spiral notebook:** You use them for schoolwork . . . why not fill the pages with your own dreams and ideas too?

- **Guided journals:** You can find themed journals on just about any topic you're interested in . . . travel, reading, cuisine, fitness, spirituality. Guided journals give you suggestions for ideas to explore.

- **Drawing pad:** Who says a journal has to be comprised solely of writing? If you're an artist or like to doodle, you can journal in a sketch pad and fill its pages with your own artistic expression.

- **Scrapbooks:** Many people have scrapbooks or photo albums that double as journals, and they fill the pages with pictures, memory keepsakes, and writing about the significance of the items in the book.

- **Word processing document:** If you prefer the sound of fingers on a keyboard over the scribble of pen on paper, a free way to log your thoughts is to type your journal in a word processing program like Microsoft Word. If you type faster than you write, computer journaling can be a quick way to release your innermost thoughts. Plus, you can password protect your diary, even on a shared computer.

Why Journaling Works

When you begin recording your perspective about life into your journal, the results can be almost magical. The very act of assigning concrete words to random thoughts floating around in your head can bring instant clarity to most situations—the truth somehow floats to the surface. Beyond that, keeping a journal can help you to:

- clear your mind

- express your emotions in a healthy way

- gain perspective about things going on in your life

- expand your creativity

What to Write About

If you ask ten different people to describe what they write about in their journals, you'd likely get ten very different answers. Me? I typically write what are called "morning pages." I was introduced to the idea in Julia Cameron's inspirational book *The Artist's Way*. In her book, Julia defines morning pages as three pages handwritten first thing every morning. The content of the pages can be absolutely anything—the goal is write "stream of consciousness," meaning you should let the content flow out of you, with no edits, no revisions, and no judgments. Morning pages clear your head and release thoughts that can block your creativity. Morning pages aren't about the quality of your writing—they're about getting all your muddled thoughts out of your head so you can make room for new inspiration.

When I first began writing morning pages, new inspiration was exactly what I needed. What I wrote about depended on my mood—sometimes I described situations that were frustrating me or stressing me out; other times I reflected on what happened the day before. No matter what I chose to write about, a few weeks into writing these morning pages, I realized I was starting to feel less stressed and more focused.

Whether you want to write morning pages or create your own routine for journaling, you can use your writing to:

- **vent your frustration**, anger, or annoyance about a situation

- **reflect on things** that have happened to you, giving you a chance to analyze and get perspective, or just release your thoughts somewhere

- **come up with a plan** for the forthcoming day and set mini-goals for everything you hope to accomplish

- **visualize and dream** about the future you want to create for yourself

- **ruminate** over stressful situations or problems you need to solve and come up with creative solutions

One last thought: When you've filled up an entire journal or diary, put it somewhere for safekeeping. Someday, looking back at things you wrote might be a great source of comfort and perspective.

10 STRESS-RELIEVING JOURNAL EXPERIMENTS

Need a little help getting started? Here are ten ideas for ways to use your journal to relieve the stress in your life:

1. **Plan for the Day:** Write in your journal first thing in the morning about the things you hope to accomplish that day. Come up with a plan for how you hope to tackle your tasks, and end your entry with a commitment to give it your best shot.

2. **Letter to Your Younger Self:** Think about a challenging situation you went through in the past, and write a letter to your "younger self" as if she were still going through the challenge. Comfort her and let her know that the situation turned out okay and explain how things worked out—it will be a good reminder to your "current self" that you can get through whatever challenges you face.

3. **Problem Solve:** Describe a problem or challenge you're experiencing and brainstorm two or three possible solutions to the situation. For each potential solution, think about the best-case scenario and the worst-case scenario of that solution. When you're done, one of the solutions might clearly be the one to try.

4. **Getaway:** Who says you have to actually leave town to experience the benefits of a getaway? Close your eyes, think about your perfect getaway destination, and go on a vacation in your journal. Write about your getaway and use all your senses in your description: *Where are you? What is the scenery like? What does the weather feel like? What does the food taste like? What kinds of people do you meet?* The

more details you can dream up, the more real your getaway will become.

5. **Daily Recap:** The opposite of morning pages, a daily recap is writing in detail about the events of the day and reflecting on your emotions and experiences in relation to them.

6. **Inspiration:** Think of someone who inspires you and describe what it is about him or her you admire. *What traits does this person have that you would like to see in yourself?*

7. **Calm Collage:** Go through old magazines and catalogs and cut out pictures, images, and words that capture the mood of calmness and serenity. Then create a collage in your journal or on a big piece of paper using these images. In the future, when you're feeling particularly stressed, just look at your "calm collage," take a deep breath, and let the stress seep out of your body.

8. **Dream Journal:** Keep your journal next to your bed and, as soon as you wake up in the morning, jot down any memories of your dreams from the night before. Since dreams are a reflection of your subconscious, explore what you think the hidden meaning of your dreams might be. Be creative!

9. **Affirm Yourself:** Come up with a positive, calming affirmation and write it down in your journal one hundred times. For example, try writing: *I am a peaceful, balanced person who knows how to deal with stress* a hundred times. By the time you're done, you'll believe your affirmation is true (and your wrist might hurt). As an alternative, keep a journal where you write (just once) one new affirmation each day!

10. **Be Someone Else:** Write about a stressful situation from another person's perspective. If you're having friendship or family challenges, try stepping into your friend's or family member's head and writing from his or her point of view. When you're through, you'll have more clarity and a better understanding of the stressful situation.

Making It Stick

Unless and until writing in your journal becomes second nature, you may find yourself forgetting to take the time to do it, especially when school and life get hectic. Here are some ideas for supporting your journaling habit:

- **Set your alarm twenty minutes earlier than usual** so you can get up and write morning pages, and **keep your journal next to your bed** or propped up against your alarm clock so you'll be reminded of your plan first thing.

- **Keep a journal or notebook in your backpack** at all times. When you find yourself with a few minutes to spare (sitting on the bus, waiting for a ride home from track practice), you can whip it out and do a quick download.

- **Buy a journal and pen that you love** so you'll be more inspired to write.

- **Don't worry if you skip writing in your journal for days, weeks, or even months.** Many people's journals have gaps in them, reflecting times when they got sidetracked or life got too busy. Start up again when you're able to and don't worry about the time that's lapsed.

Do you know what each of these famous diary writers inked about? See how many you can match up correctly:

1. Anne Frank

2. Samuel Pepys

3. Kurt Cobain

4. Frida Kahlo

5. Bridget Jones

6. Freedom Writers

7. Elie Wiesel

8. Richard Wagner

9. Zlata Filipović

10. Sylvia Plath

A. This Englishman kept a diary from 1660 to 1669. Now that it's published, it has become famous for the detail it offers about the English Restoration period and interesting eyewitness accounts of famous historical events.

B. This famous artist's diary is filled with watercolors, sketches, love letters, and an insider's look at her relationship with husband and artist Diego Rivera.

C. This eleven-year-old diarist wrote about life in war-torn Sarajevo in the 1990s. She donated the proceeds of her book to start a charity to benefit child victims of the Bosnian war.

D. This famous composer's diary was published in German with the name *Das Braune Buch* or *The Brown Book*.

E. His diary about his experiences in a concentration camp as a teenager became the published book *Night*, which Oprah made famous when she selected it for her book club.

F. This fictional diarist writes in detail about her calorie counts, her cigarette and alcoholic beverage intake, her short skirts, and her quest for love.

G. Though she started keeping journals at the age of eleven, this famous poet's adult journals, which she began in 1950 as a freshman at Smith College, were eventually published.

H. This music icon of the 1990s published a collection of letters, scribbled notes, drawings, and other personal writing in a book called *Journals*.

I. This group of high school students from Southern California journaled about their struggles to persevere despite living in communities full of poverty, drugs, and gangs.

J. Her diary tells the story of her twenty-five months living in hiding in Amsterdam during the Holocaust. Since it was published in 1947, it has become one of the most widely read books in the world.

ANSWERS: 1-J, 2-A, 3-H, 4-B, 5-F, 6-I, 7-E, 8-D, 9-C, 10-G

Dear Debbie,

I am in foster care and have lived in a group home for two years . . . long enough, I'd say. I've been hoping for a family, and we may have found one, but I'm worried about whether or not it is the right one. How can I deal with my stress when it pops up?

Miranda, age 14

Dear Miranda,

Writing about your concerns in a journal would be a great way to unload and release all your fears, anxieties, and stresses when it comes to the uncertainty of your future. As you write in your journal, let it all out. Every thought, good and bad; every fear, real and imaginary; every hope, big and small. Treat your diary like a best friend and don't worry about being judged or questioned as you release your thoughts. This may be a stressful time for you, but writing about your feelings will help you stop stress from getting the best of you. I hope your situation works out exactly as you dream it will!

XOXO Debbie

WHAT JESS DOES

"One thing I do to de-stress and relax is write nonstop for ten minutes in my journal. I don't lift the pen up from the page— whatever comes out, comes out. It is freeing!"

—Jess Weiner, Actionist

TIME-OUT:
SOCIAL MEDIA SURVIVAL GUIDE

You are part of the first generation of teens to grow up with social media, so it only makes sense that you're also on the front lines of figuring out how to navigate the stressors that come along with playing in the virtual Wild West.

Sure, interacting on social media has many tangible benefits, including:

- the ability to connect with people you might not otherwise have access to (exchanging tweets with a famous filmmaker or reaching out to one of your sheroes to get a quote for a class assignment)

- a sense of camaraderie and belonging around important social, political, and pop culture events (live-tweeting the season premier of your favorite TV show or joining in an online celebration over a presidential election)

- an easy way to stay in contact with friends you might otherwise lose touch with (old camp buddies or friends who moved out of state or country)

- the opportunity to create your own personal "brand" for who you are as a student, a college applicant, an entrepreneur, a blogger, or anything else you want to be

Yet, though the plusses are many, it's no secret that maintaining an online presence comes with more than a few emotional challenges, like:

- becoming overly concerned about how others perceive you

- feeling pressure to look cool or pretty or popular or interesting

- dealing with negative comments and harmful, hurtful behavior from others online

- falling into the "compare and despair" trap by hyperfocusing on how "perfect" everyone else's life seems to be in comparison with yours

- saying good-bye to a little thing called "privacy"

The good news is, it's possible to have a less stressful and more balanced relationship with social media. All it takes is making a conscious choice to conduct yourself online in a respectful way—respect for you, for your friends, and for everyone else who might view what you do. Here's how:

Don't overshare. Though some people might be compelled to share every little detail of their lives online (down to how many rolls they had with dinner or how long they brushed their teeth that night), *you* get to choose what you want to put out into the world. To know when a status update, tweet, or pic is oversharing, check in with your gut before hitting the post button. If you get a feeling of hesitation, uncertainty, or a hint of the ick factor, hit cancel. What might seem good to share in a moment of impulse could leave you feeling vulnerable or embarrassed down the road.

Remember that no one's life is perfect. People only share what they want others to see, so it's no wonder this tends to be the great stuff, like highlights from a dream vacation or perfectly lit and posed selfies. Absorbing everyone else's great news and personal victories can make us feel like our lives suck in comparison. View others' posts and pictures with a grain of salt. *Everyone* has stuff going on in their life that is challenging and difficult. We just don't always see it.

Keep relationship status private. Ups and downs in relationships and painful breakups are hard enough to go through without the whole world being in your business. Avoid labeling your relationships on social media so you don't have to go through public scrutiny should your relationship status change.

Practice respect online, both to yourself and to others. If there is a golden rule of social media, it would be this: treat others online the way you would like to be treated. If you want your social media platforms to be safe environments where you get to virtually engage with others in a fun, positive way, make sure your comments and interactions with others have the same tone.

Set clear boundaries. Decide what behavior is and isn't okay in your virtual world and then stick to those boundaries no matter what. Unfriend or block people when they interact with you in a way that doesn't feel good. Remember, this is *your* social media life. You get to decide what it looks and feels like. If lines are crossed and you're being bullied online, follow these two rules: 1) don't retaliate, and 2) get help. Cyberbullying can escalate quickly and leave devastation in its wake. Turn to a trusted mentor or other adult for guidance on how to protect yourself and best resolve the situation.

Keep your social media life in balance with everything else. If you find you're spending a lot of time on social media to the detriment of other things in your life, get back on track by going on a social media hiatus. Like cutting carbs or gluten from your diet, taking a break from social media can help you reset your online habits in a positive way.

10
ZONING OUT
AND TUNING IN

When life gets too stressful and the pressure's on, sometimes the thing you need most is the thing you think you just can't do: *take a day off . . . from everything.*

If you're going a hundred miles an hour trying to balance all your relationships, classes, and obligations, something's going to suffer. Unfortunately, that something often ends up being your spirit.

So whether you can take off a day, a week, or only a few hours, setting aside time to zone out, tune in, and reconnect with yourself can bring much-needed balance back into your life.

ZONING OUT AND TUNING IN: Taking care of yourself by setting aside the time to nurture your mind, body, and soul. Ideal for reducing stress related to:

- being overscheduled and overwhelmed
- facing impossible deadlines
- having too many obligations
- feeling as though you're on the brink of a breakdown
- having the sense that your life is out of balance

Tuning In 101

One of my best friends, Renée Adams, is a spiritual life coach, which means that she teaches others how to tune in and reconnect so they can live more fulfilled lives. I asked Renée how teens can begin the process of tuning in to de-stress. "Tuning in begins with turning down the volume on the rest of life. That means turning down your iPod, the TV, your friends, your parents, your teachers, your coaches, and even your own negative chatter," Renée explained.

When you take the time to check in with yourself like this, you can usually tell if you're out of sync, because you'll feel:

- anxious

- like you're always in a hurry

- like you need a change

- dissatisfied

- chaotic

On the other hand, when you're *in sync*, or connected to what's going on inside, you'll probably feel:

- loving

- patient

- like you enjoy being in the moment

- as if you can see the beauty in things

- like your mind and body are "quiet"

- full of gratitude

Tuning in is key to reducing stress and creating a more balanced, peaceful you. As Renée describes it, it's a form of "self-care" related to that whole idea that you can't take care of anyone—boyfriend, girlfriend, BFF, family, the kids you babysit for—unless and until you take care of yourself.

Self-care involves nurturing the four areas of your being:

1. **Physical:** Being well-rested and well-nourished, flexible, and taking care of personal hygiene needs (like putting on sunscreen, getting nails done, taking a bath, etc.).

2. **Mental:** Practicing positive "self-talk," avoiding violence in TV and video games, looking for uplifting sources of encouragement.

3. **Emotional:** Having healthy ways to release emotions, such as going to the woods and screaming, journaling, hitting your mattress with a plastic bat, cranking up the music, exercising.

4. **Spiritual:** Finding a space for yourself such as nature or your room or a place of worship to pray or meditate, read inspiring literature, and so on.

HOW BALANCED ARE YOU?

Sometimes it's easier to figure out where your life is out of balance when you see the cold, hard facts on paper. To do this, Renée suggests making a balance wheel. Start by writing down all the different aspects of your life that take up your time and energy—things you love, things you hate, things you wish you could spend more time doing. Your list might look something like this:

- Friends

- School

- Family

- After-school job

- Hobbies

- Exercise

- Chilling

- Clubs

Once you've written your list, grab a piece of paper and draw a large circle on it. Then view your circle like a pie and draw lines to create "slices" for each item in your list. The size of each slice should reflect how much time and energy you spend on the item. The more time and energy spent, the bigger the slice.

Here's what a balance wheel based on the above list might look like:

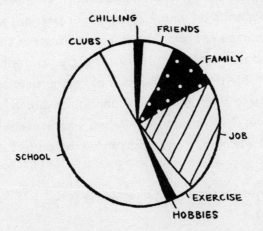

See what I mean? When you put things down on paper, sometimes you can see what's really going on. And with the above example, it's pretty clear that things are seriously out of balance. You deserve to take care of yourself by making the slight adjustments that can help you reconfigure your balance wheel for the better. The goal isn't to make each piece of the pie the same size, but to make each slice fit more closely with how things would be divided up in your perfect world.

Of course, some pieces of your pie are mandatory and can't be changed (like school!), so focus your energy on the areas you *do* have control over. Renée suggests you find out what invigorates you and recharges your batteries . . . the things that, when you're doing them, you're so into them you lose track of time. Then find a way to weave those things into your life or have them be a bigger slice of your pie!

Reconnecting

When you notice you're lacking balance in your life, it's time to commit to doing something about it. What exactly the "it" is depends on your interests, your passion, and what feeds your soul. I should mention that sometimes what you need is to spend quality time by yourself. I know many people don't like the idea of "alone time" because it may make them feel lonely, unpopular, bored, or all of the above. But consider this—when you're overscheduled and overwhelmed, alone time can be the perfect antidote, because it:

- restores your energy and recharges you

- gives you a true break from the stress of daily life
- helps you become more confident in your abilities and who you are

Whether you're spending quality time alone or with a close friend, ensuring that you're nurturing the different areas of your life is what's important. Says Renée, "Give yourself permission to tune in . . . you can't afford not to."

TEN THINGS TO HELP YOU RECONNECT

Here are ten ideas for how to zone out, reconnect, and get going with the business of finding balance in your life.

1. **Rent a movie.** There's nothing like a little escapism to instantly transport you to another world where your stress doesn't exist. Rent movies that inspire you, stir your spirit, and keep you connected to the ideas that make you feel most alive.

2. **Go to a museum.** Getting inspiration from the artistic masters, past and present, can help you tap into your creative side and think about different approaches for handling your stress.

3. **Volunteer.** There's no better way to put your stressful life in perspective than by devoting a few hours or an afternoon to helping out with a favorite cause. (See page 121 for more on volunteering as a way to put things into perspective.)

4. **Pamper yourself.** Finding time for a massage, facial, pedicure, haircut, or even a long bath reminds you that taking care of your well-being is a priority.

5. **Go for a hike.** Wear comfortable shoes, grab an energy bar and some water, and *walk, walk, walk.* With each step, you'll pound out some stress and do something great for your body at the same time.

6. **Read a book.** Curl up on the couch, pull up your grandma's crocheted afghan, and dive into a book (*not* a textbook or schoolwork).

7. **Spend quality time with your friends or family.** Take the day off from stress and go shopping with Mom or go to the beach with some friends. After all, isn't spending time with the ones we love what life is all about, anyway?

8. **Listen to your favorite album.** Charge up your iPod, pop in the headphones, and tune in by zoning out with some music. Music can instantly transform your mood and outlook.

9. **Take a nap** (*one of my favorite ways to disconnect in order to reconnect!*). Even a short nap can do wonders for helping you feel more together and grounded. If you're struggling with a problem, try asking the universe for a solution before you drift off to sleep. You just might wake up with your answer!

10. **Go through your pictures and make a new scrapbook or photo album.** Sometimes reflecting on who you were and what you've been through reminds you of the person you are today and the things that matter the most to you.

Going Zen

Millions of people around the world practice yoga, meditation, and visualization to stay calm, focused, and positive, no matter how hectic or intense life gets. By weaving a few of these stress-reducing techniques rooted in Eastern philosophy into your life, you can find serenity in just about any storm.

Become a Yogi

Yoga uses movement, breath awareness, relaxation, and meditation techniques to create balance between the mind and the body. Classes typically include quiet meditation time, deep stretches with a focus on body alignment, strengthening poses, tuning in and focusing on your breathing, and a series of strenuous movements. Depending on the type of yoga, your class might feel like an aerobics class, while more traditional classes might focus primarily on breathing.

To track down a yoga studio near you, visit the website Yoga Finder (www.yogafinder.com), where you can search for yoga studios by city. Don't forget to check with your local YMCA or YWCA as well, since many offer yoga classes as part of their fitness programs.

Related to yoga and just as powerful when it comes to feeling centered is meditation, which is a formal way of tuning out the outside world and focusing inward. Even though meditation has its roots in ancient Eastern religions, it is practiced by people of all faiths around the world, as well as people with no religious affiliation.

Meditation is about connecting with your breath and your awareness, and it requires nothing more than a comfortable, quiet place, a few minutes of your time, and the ability to tune out the outside world while focusing inward (this last step is easier said than done). Your mind may wander while you're meditating, and that's fine (and normal). Simply acknowledge the thought and return your focus to your breath. Meditation gets easier with practice, so start out slowly and be patient with yourself!

Visualize

Visualizing can be a powerful tool when it comes to creating or manifesting positive outcomes for challenging situations. In a way, visualization is an example of the "power of positive thinking" in action. By focusing good energy on your stressful situations and visualizing positive resolutions, you'll feel more hopeful, which will ultimately lead to a more balanced, peaceful you.

The next time you're super stressed out about a situation that's out of your control, close your eyes and visualize the ideal outcome. Use this vision in your meditation by putting your energy toward manifesting your perfect resolution.

Got Five Minutes? Try These Zen Time-outs

- **Five-minute meditation:** You don't have to sit on a mountain and contemplate the meaning of life for a week to calm your spirit. Find a quiet, peaceful place where you can comfortably sit upright, close your eyes, and focus on your breathing and your breath. Inhale through your nose, exhale slowly through your mouth, and clear your mind.

- **Savasana (Corpse Pose):** Lie flat on your back with arms to the side and legs slightly apart and relax every inch of your body—from your largest leg muscles to the tiniest muscle in your forehead. Tune in to your body to discover where you're holding tension and release it.

- **Viparita Karani (Legs-Up-the-Wall Pose):** Lie on your back with your butt up against a wall and your legs sticking up alongside the wall at a ninety-degree angle. Arms should be loosely at your side, eyes are closed, and your breathing relaxed. Do this for five minutes for a quick recharge.

- **Relaxation breathing:** Find a comfortable chair or sit upright on the floor, close your eyes, and inhale deeply and slowly through your nose, while letting your lungs fill up with air (your belly should stick out as you inhale). Hold the air in your lungs for a count to five, and then slowly exhale through your mouth, using your diaphragm muscle to push the air out and pulling your belly button inward as far as it can go. Repeat ten times.

- **Visualization vacation:**
Find a quiet place (or
pop in your earphones
and turn on your iPod),
close your eyes, and
visualize a place or a
moment in time when
you felt happy, calm,
serene, and loved. Go to
this place in your mind
by visualizing all the
rich details, giving in to the sensations so you can
experience the feelings that go along with it.

Making It Stick

Tuning in is something people need to consciously remember to do every day, and it may take time, maybe even years, for it to become a regular habit. Here are some suggestions for making this important approach to stress relief stick:

- **Every morning, consciously make the choice to tune in to your emotional, mental, spiritual, and physical needs.** Write out this commitment and tape it to your mirror or laminate it and hang it in the shower so the words are one of the first things you see each morning.

- **Be aware of the things you already do to take care of yourself.** It's comforting to realize you're already doing many things that are self-nurturing (i.e., playing an instrument, participating in a sports team, praying, etc.).

- When things get to be too much and you feel like you're spiraling out of control, **stop and give yourself five minutes to breathe,** catch up with your spirit, and listen to what's in your head and heart.

JOURNAL IT:

- **Write a list of five to ten things you can do to make you feel good about yourself.** This could be anything from going for a run or eating a healthy meal to doing karaoke with your friends—there are no right or wrong answers. Once you've created your list, copy it onto an index card or small piece of paper that you can keep in your wallet or purse as a reminder that the tools for reconnecting are at your fingertips.

- **Dedicate twenty minutes each week to writing about your hopes and dreams.** *What are your fears? What are your wildest dreams? When are you most yourself? What makes you feel most content? Don't censor yourself . . . just let it flow.* Writing about your innermost dreams will bring you one step closer to making them a reality.

Do you make keeping your life in balance a priority?

1. You've got two weeks to get prepped for finals, so you cut out all social obligations and TV time until your deadlines have passed.

   a. *Totally me*

   b. *Could be me*

   c. *Not me*

2. You're completely wiped out, but you can't justify a Sunday afternoon nap, so you grab a double espresso to keep yourself going.

   a. *Totally me*

   b. *Could be me*

   c. *Not me*

3. You manage to find time for a run, but instead of zoning out with some tunes, you cue up your iPod to a recording of a lecture from class.

   a. *Totally me*

   b. *Could be me*

   c. *Not me*

4. You haven't read a book for pleasure in the past six months.

   a. *Totally me*

   b. *Could be me*

   c. *Not me*

5. When life gets especially stressful, "self-indulgent" things like long showers, combing your hair, or getting a pedicure go right out the window.

   a. *Totally me*

   b. *Could be me*

   c. *Not me*

SCORING

Mostly As: You're an all-or-nothing kind of gal and could benefit from more balance in your life.

Mostly Bs: You know how to find balance, but you don't always remember to make it a priority.

Mostly Cs: You appreciate the importance of tuning in and creating balance in your life.

CREATE A TUNING-IN AFFIRMATION

Once you've come up with your affirmation, write it down on an index card or piece of paper and tape it up where you'll see it often. Use one of these examples or create an affirmation of your own.

- *I am a balanced, peaceful person who knows the importance of tuning in.*

- *I give myself time to reconnect with myself and accomplish everything I choose to get done.*

- *My stress melts away when I spend the time to tune in and reconnect with myself.*

BALANCE GURU RENÉE ADAMS'S ADVICE FOR STRESSED-OUT TEENS

"Stay tuned in to yourself. Even if you think following your inner voice won't be popular, you may find that others follow your tune. When you're tuning in, you can't make a mistake. And no matter how bad your life seems, you can get back on track . . . guaranteed."

Dear Debbie,

I get stressed out by just about everything. There are constant pressures coming from every aspect of my life: my friends, the people who aren't my friends, my parents, school grades, what career I want to do for the rest of my life, sports teams, extracurricular activities. . . . How do I handle it all?

Heather, age 16

Dear Heather,

Talk about needing a day off . . . I get tired just thinking about everything you've got going on. Seriously, it sounds like you're stressing out about a whole bunch of things and might be forgetting to take time to do the things that make you feel good about you. When you're in the moment and doing things you enjoy (whether it's going to the mall with a friend, watching horror flicks, reading a book, or jamming out on your guitar), your mind is getting a much-needed break from all that worry. These little stress breaks can actually help you think about everything you've got going on from a healthier place. Try doing this for a week, and see how it works out: Every morning when you wake up, think of one thing you are going to do that day in the form of a stress break that is just for you. Then make it a priority to take that break during the day. I guarantee you'll not only see a difference in your stress levels, but you'll also feel good about the fact that you're taking such good care of your spirit. Good luck!

XOXO Debbie

WHAT KEREN DOES

"Living in the city can be a noisy, hectic experience. One thing that I love to do in the early morning hours is nurture a few plants that I have in my apartment and on my deck. I trim the leaves and branches, fertilize them, spritz them with water, and move them around to give them optimal sun. There's no deadline and no computer involved and they don't talk back! And it reminds me that I need to take the same kind of dedicated, calm approach to taking care of myself."

—Keren Taylor, Founder and Director of WriteGirl

GETTING
PHYSICAL

11

EXERCISE

I couldn't write a book about how to relieve stress and create balance without mentioning exercise—it's one of the best stress relievers around. Exercise gives you immediate relief, and making it a regular part of your life can help you maintain manageable stress levels all the time.

I realize that exercise isn't everyone's thing. In fact, I know that the very *thought* of exercising makes some people break out in a sweat. But even if that's you, stick with me. Exercise doesn't have to mean marathons and daylong tennis tournaments. Whether you want to be a CrossFit fiend and work out for hours a day or take a less intense approach, there is a type of physical activity that you can connect with to reduce your stress.

EXERCISE: Activity requiring physical exertion. Ideal for reducing stress related to:

- needing to vent

- having high expectations placed on you

- bottling up your emotions

- feeling overwhelmed

- finding yourself in the midst of an emotional spiral

- being concerned about global issues

- experiencing peer pressure

So just what qualifies as exercise, and how much do you have to do to reap the stress-relief rewards? There are two ways to think about exercise: (1) exercise as a "way of life," and (2) exercise as a quick way to release stress in a jam.

When I talk about exercise as a "way of life," I'm referring to exercise that is a regular part of your daily or weekly routine . . . the kind that's woven into your lifestyle. Technically, it means squeezing in at least thirty minutes of cardio (running, fast walking, swimming, biking) three to four times a week. If you're already doing this, then you're also already reaping significant stress-relief rewards.

Benefits of Exercise as a Way of Life

You're probably aware of the benefits of exercise from a "book knowledge" perspective, but have you ever *really* considered how exercise alleviates the stress in your life and gives you balance? Here's how.

Regular exercise benefits your **body** by:

- **Boosting your immune system,** which prevents you from getting sick. If you do get sick, your illness won't last as long (an especially important side effect, since stress actually weakens your immune system).

- **Making your body metabolize food more efficiently,** which means you'll get more energy from your diet and you won't have to rely on that second can of Red Bull.

- **Helping you sleep better** by burning off more sugar during the day and releasing more "sleep chemicals" in your body. (NOTE: Just don't exercise late in the day, or you may find that you're more wired than tired.)

- **Giving you more overall energy** so you'll be ready to handle whatever challenges come your way.

- **Releasing natural "happy pills" in your body** in the form of endorphins. These "painkilling proteins" are released in the brain during vigorous exercise and make you feel more positive and happy, even in the most stressful circumstances.

Regular exercise benefits your **mind** by:

- **Keeping you mentally healthy** so you can approach any stressful situation from a position of strength.

- **Enabling you to think more clearly,** which can help in everything from focusing better on tests and assignments to making smarter choices about how to keep all the balls you're juggling in the air.

- **Giving you the time you need to process, analyze, or zone out,** all while doing something great for yourself.

Regular exercise benefits your **soul** by:

- **Making you feel more empowered and in control,** a side effect that can trickle into all aspects of your life.

- **Boosting your self-esteem and confidence** in your abilities, which can directly translate to confidence in other areas of your life.

- **Showing you how mentally tough you are.**
  Each time you push yourself and persevere while
  exercising, you're proving to yourself that you can
  accomplish anything you set your mind to.

And if you can get your exercise fix outdoors, even better. Recent research shows that, in addition to the potential physical benefits of exercising outside versus indoors, people experience more significant psychological benefits when they get their fitness fix in nature, including feeling more happiness, vitality, and positive self-esteem, and less tension, depression, and fatigue.

Exercise for Quick Stress Relief

Even if you're not a regular exerciser experiencing the long-term benefits of a consistent fitness routine, you can still experience great results by exercising when the pressure is on.

Have you ever been so stressed and anxious that you felt like you could scream? That's the perfect time to release your negative energy in the form of sweat and exertion.

Here are some easy ways to use exercise for quick, on-the-spot stress relief:

- Jump rope as fast as you can for one minute.

- If you have access to a punching bag at school or in the gym, practice your "one-two" punch for five minutes.

- Run five short sprints, giving yourself time to recover in between.

- Grab your bike and ride it up a big hill with as much power, strength, and speed as you can.

Finding the Time

It might not make logical sense, but when you're so stressed out that you barely have time to breathe, let alone hit the gym, that's exactly when taking a break to exercise can benefit you the most.

I'm not saying this to add one more thing to your constantly growing "to do" list. But if you can find the time to squeeze in even a *little* physical fitness, the resulting stress-relief benefits will make that time incredibly well spent. Here is how working out can help you *work things out*:

- Strenuous exercise releases endorphins into your body, giving you an instant emotional and mental boost.

- By setting aside time to exercise, you're investing in yourself and acknowledging that you're worth it (and you are!).

- Exercise gives your brain a much-needed break from studying, planning, and stressing.

If you're not on a sports team and you're already overbooked, how can you find the time to squeeze in some cardio to get the blood flowing? Here are some ideas.

If you have no time for exercise:

- Choose the stairs over the elevator or escalator any chance you get.

- Walk or bike instead of taking the bus or getting a ride.

- Anytime you're walking (to class, home after school, at the mall), walk with a purpose (fast, strong, and powerful).

If you have ten minutes:

- Go for a brisk walk around the block.

- Put on a CD of your favorite dance tunes and break a sweat in your living room.

- Alternate jumping rope with sit-ups during a study break in your bedroom.

If you have twenty minutes:

- Go for a twenty-minute jog around the neighborhood or on the track after school.

- Offer to ride your bike to run an errand.

- Flip through an issue of *Seventeen* or *Shape* and try out all the exercises in the fitness section.

If you have thirty minutes:

- Run for a half hour around the neighborhood or on the track after school.

- Grab some light hand weights (cans of soup or bottles of water will work just as well) and do alternating bicep curls, triceps lifts, squats, and shoulder presses while watching TV.

- Pop in an exercise DVD (you can rent these from your local library) and create your own at-home gym.

Making It Stick

If you want to make exercise a regular part of your life no matter how busy you get, keep these tips in mind:

- Even **five minutes of cardio** can do wonders for clearing your head.

- **Give yourself a break** if you skip out on exercise because you're too swamped. Stressing over why you didn't exercise won't do any good, but making a choice to start over with your routine the following day will.

- **Combine exercise with other de-stressing techniques:** Listen to music while working out or combine your fitness routine with bonding time with a friend or pet.

JOURNAL IT:

- **Jot down a list of five things that you like about exercise** and the way it makes you feel (preferably do this shortly after you've exercised and while you're experiencing the emotional benefits). When you're feeling unmotivated or like it's not worth it, go back and reread what you wrote to remember why exercise is so good for your body, mind, and soul.

- **Write down a goal of one thing you can change in your weekly routine** to further incorporate exercise into your life (i.e., walk home from school once a week instead of taking the bus, do push-ups and sit-ups during commercial breaks while watching TV, etc.)

Quiz

What workout style suits your personality? Answer these questions to find out!

1. If I were to spend a whole Saturday morning exercising by myself, I would be most likely to . . .

    a. *grab some water and an energy bar and go for a hike.*

    b. *compete in a road race.*

    c. *participate in an Ultimate Frisbee tournament.*

    d. *go to a yoga retreat.*

2. When it's time for PE at school, I . . .

    a. *hope we're not stuck in the gym.*

    b. *try to beat my high scores in the Presidential Fitness Challenge.*

    c. *spend as much time chatting along the sidelines as I do shooting hoops.*

    d. *opt to run laps instead of playing badminton.*

3. If I were to aspire to be a professional athlete, it would be as . . .

    a. *a triathlete.*

    b. *a basketball player.*

    c. *a cheerleader.*

    d. *a body builder.*

4. When I'm on vacation, I'm most likely to fit in my exercise by . . .

    a. *doing whatever the environment lends itself to (i.e., snorkeling, diving, hiking).*

    b. *working out in the gym and sticking to my exercise schedule.*

    c. *joining in a pickup soccer game.*

    d. *exploring my vacation spot alone on my bike.*

5. When it comes to after-school sports, the one most my speed is . . .

    a. *cross-country.*

    b. *tennis.*

    c. *golf.*

    d. *yoga and meditation.*

So what's your workout style?

Mostly As: Outdoorsy Gal
You love the feel of the sun on your skin and fresh air in your lungs, and you're game for just about any type of physical activity as long as you're not stuck indoors. Try: hiking, mountain climbing, trail running, adventure racing, surfing, skiing, snowshoeing, kayaking.

Mostly Bs: Competitive Coed
You are most happy exercising when the stakes are high and you're working out to win. Try: tennis, volleyball, field hockey, basketball, track and field, swimming.

Mostly Cs: Social Bee
For you, hang-out time with friends and the social aspect of a sport are just as important as the fitness side effects. Try: golf, softball, cheerleading, soccer, beach volleyball, Frisbee, rowing.

Mostly Ds: Solo Suzie
Tuning in and recharging with healthy alone time is what makes exercise and staying fit so important for you. Try: yoga, running, aikido, bodybuilding, Pilates, ice-skating.

CREATE AN EXERCISE AFFIRMATION

Write it down on an index card or piece of paper and post it where you'll see it often. Here are a few examples of exercise affirmations:

- *When I exercise, I am giving myself the gift of fitness and clarity.*

- *By choosing to exercise, I am choosing to create balance in my life.*

- *Exercise brings me peace, happiness, and the time to reflect.*

GET INSPIRED

Need a little inspiration to tap into the exercise goddess within? Check out one of these movies:

Bend It Like Beckham (2002)

Blue Crush (2002)

Love & Basketball (2000)

Dear Debbie,

I'm like many teens I know. I'm always striving to meet the expectations of the people in my life. I feel like families, friends, and the media are always describing how teens should be, and then when we don't meet their criteria, it leaves us feeling like failures. How can I avoid this kind of stress or get rid of it when I have it?

Sophie, age 16

Dear Sophie,

There's nothing worse than trying to live up to expectations placed on you by others, especially when they're not even grounded in reality. These types of stresses can certainly deal a big blow to your self-esteem, and that makes it harder to be in a place of strength to handle all the challenges of being a teenager. You may want to try incorporating exercise into your everyday life. By exercising—running, walking, biking, swimming, whatever—you are doing something positive for you that has some pretty amazing side effects, including boosting your self-esteem. When you're feeling empowered and good about yourself, you'll be less likely to care what others think of you. You'll be living up to your own expectations of being a strong, independent, motivated young woman, and there's absolutely nothing stressful about that. Good luck!

XOXO Debbie

TIPS FOR EXERCISING WITH A FRIEND

Social time + exercise = a win-win situation for everyone involved! Here are some tips for getting healthy and reducing stress with a friend:

- **Make it a date.** Make regular exercise dates so you and your friend(s) can look forward to the social time together (i.e., swimming together every Sunday afternoon, running together on Thursday nights, walking and chatting after school on Tuesdays). Even an hour a week would be great!

- **Sign up with a club or organization.** Join a running club, biking club, or other sports organization, either with a friend or to make new ones! You'll likely find they host group workouts and other social activities.

- **Take a class together.** Sign up for yoga or take a kickboxing class together. By adding structure to your workout, you'll be less likely to skip out on it.

- **Make it fun.** Plan social outings to tie in with your workout. For example, go for a trail run and then have a picnic, or plan a bike ride that ends at a fabulous place for brunch!

- **Leave the competition at home.** Even if you and your friend are competitive about everything, ditch the rivalry and make exercising together about being healthy, having fun, and connecting with each other.

FIND OUT MORE

The Women's Sports Foundation (www.womenssportsfoundation.org) is an organization aimed at advancing the lives of girls and women through sports and physical activity. Here you'll find information on every sport imaginable—from archery to snowboarding—including a breakdown of the equipment you'll need, the costs involved, and where to find classes near you.

WHAT BRIDGET DOES

"As I work in a very stressful environment, and given that I'm a mom of a seventeen-month-old with little time to myself outside work, I employ a variety of stress-reducing tactics depending on the situation, including my favorite—getting out in nature by going for a hike or even (and this is harder to pull off) going for an overnight camping excursion with the family and dogs."

—Bridget Perry, executive

TIME-OUT:
BODY IMAGE REBOOT

Jump on YouTube and search for celebrity retouching and you'll find thousands of videos showing exactly how Photoshop wizards do their magic—take a few inches off the waist, thighs, and arms, plump up the breasts, elongate the neck, and let's not forget eliminate any trace of wrinkles, blemishes, or pores.

Yet despite the fact that the curtain has been pulled back and we know most of the media images we see aren't actually *real*, poor body image continues to be a huge problem among young girls and teens (and women, for that matter!).

Here are a couple of significant statistics, courtesy of the National Eating Disorders Association (NEDA):

- 81 percent of ten-year-olds are afraid of being fat

- two-thirds of middle school and high school girls say their vision of an ideal body is influenced by what they see in magazines

- half of these girls say the images they see make them want to lose weight

So what does this have to do with stress? Well, as it turns out, there is a direct link between negative body image and stress. In fact, being overly concerned about body image can morph into body dysmorphic disorder (BDD), a mental condition marked by obsession with what one sees as their appearance "flaws." But even if body dissatisfaction doesn't reach the level of BDD, it still has negative side effects. Studies show that teenage girls who struggle with their body image are more likely to be depressed, anxious, and suicidal than their peers who feel good about their bodies.

So how to deal?

There's no quick fix to the body image blues, but you can make changes in your habits and life that will reduce the impact of stressful self-image thoughts. Here's how:

Limit exposure to media images that make you feel bad. I love flipping through fashion or gossip magazines as much as the next girl, but sometimes seeing all those super-skinny, scantily-clad models posing in the latest styles or devouring a "who wore it best" spread comparing two celebs pushes me over the edge. Before I know it, I'm scrutinizing, analyzing, and wishing I looked a little more like the girls in the photos. If you're like me, take notice of what kind of media makes you feel crappy and then limit the time you spend looking at that media. You might even consider doing a "media fast" for thirty days. You'd be surprised at just how much better you'll feel about yourself when you cut back on consuming those images.

Make a list of your role models and their traits that you admire. When you think about the people you aspire to be like someday, my hunch is that very few of the qualities that make your list will have anything to do with what size jeans she wears or how perfectly shaped her nose is. More than likely, you'll be writing down qualities like generosity or intelligence or creativity or kindness. People are special to us because of *who they are*, not what they look like. So why not appreciate yourself in the same way?

Notice and end negative self-talk. How many times do you talk about how fat you are or how big your butt is or how you wish your waist or thighs were smaller? Talking badly about our bodies is practically an epidemic, and it's contagious to boot. Women and girls tend to feed off the negative self-talk of others and feel the need to join in. But you don't have to. Make the decision to stop the negative self-talk cycle by 1) noticing it when you or others do it, 2) not participating in it, and 3) speaking out against it.

Soak in positive, inspirational media. There are plenty of books and videos out there that exist to counter the negative media images we are bombarded with. To get started, check out Caitlin Boyle's book *Operation Beautiful: Transforming the Way You See Yourself One Post-it Note at a Time,* watch the DOVE self-esteem building videos like *Evolution, Onslaught, Real Beauty Sketches,* and *Selfies,* and spend some time checking out We Stop Hate's inspiring teen-created videos (www.westophate.com).

Create your own positive body image affirmations. Remember—what you focus on becomes how you feel. Write some affirmations that focus on what you love about yourself, what you're ridiculously good at, what your favorite features are, and what qualities you're most proud of. Then read those affirmations each and every day.

12

NUTRITION

You probably know all about the do's and don'ts when it comes to nutrition. I'll bet you could draw the food pyramid in your sleep, have been appropriately warned about the perils of too much sugar, and know the importance of drinking eight glasses of water each day. But would you believe that eating seven bananas a day will reduce your stress levels by 75 percent? Okay, that one's not really true. But it is no joke that your nutrition can have a direct impact on how well your body stands up to emotional and physical stress. Too much or too little of something can cause your body to be at a nutritional disadvantage and not as able to help you deflect your stress. When it comes to nutrition, it's all about—what else—*balance*.

PRACTICING GOOD NUTRITION: Making conscious choices to eat a balanced and healthy diet, with the goal of achieving nutritional well-being. Ideal for reducing stress related to:

- experiencing chronic stress
- pulling late nights prepping for a test
- struggling with self-identity and body image
- coping with the physical side effects of all stressors
- feeling down or depressed

On a good day, I approach food as if it's fuel—something I ingest not only to enjoy, but to help my body run efficiently. On a stressed-out day, the whole "food as fuel" thing often flies out the window. Instead, I have a tendency to treat food like it's a comfort and distraction in disguise. And of course, it's on really stressful days that it's more important than ever to practice good nutrition, especially because stress and nutrition are intricately intertwined. Here's how:

- When your body is releasing the stress hormones adrenaline and cortisol, **you feel hungry even if you really aren't.**

- **Many people overeat when they're stressed out,** which can make them feel sluggish and tired.

- **Stress can interfere with your digestive system,** resulting in uncomfortable side effects like constipation.

- **Some people skip meals** when they're anxious, which causes a drop in the body's blood sugar levels and reduces its ability to manage stress.

When you're already feeling like you're getting it from all sides, the last thing you need is for your body to be working against you just because you made a bad choice in the cafeteria. Luckily, there are simple ways to keep your body nutritionally prepped to help you think more clearly, have better focus, and "be in shape" when it comes to handling stress.

Do you take the "anything goes" nutritional approach when you're feeling really stressed out? Do you slip into "food survival mode," where the only thing you're concerned with is eating to get through the next minute, hour, or day? If so, unfortunately, your body often responds in the exact opposite way than you were hoping for. Here are some examples of how dietary choices might negatively impact you.

THE PROBLEM: EATING EXTREMES

When people respond to stress with extreme eating, it's usually in one of two ways: overeating and bingeing, or skipping out on meals altogether. Neither option is a good one.

When stressed-out people overeat, it's generally because they are searching for comfort or relief in that third helping of dinner or the pint of Ben & Jerry's before bedtime. But even if overeating or bingeing makes you feel better in the moment, that comfort is short-lived. Overeating always feels bad after the fact: You're left bloated and uncomfortable, sluggish, unmotivated, and guilty.

Skipping meals isn't any better. Forgoing food will slow down your metabolism, as well as give you headaches, make you feel flaky, and cause you to have trouble concentrating.

Both overeating and skipping meals wreak havoc on blood sugar levels in your body, since these levels rise and fall depending on how much you ingest. When your blood sugar's too high, you might feel wired and anxious, and when it's too low, you might feel tired and sluggish.

The Remedy: If you're prone to eating extremes, balance things out by "grazing" or eating small meals and snacks throughout the day so you don't get food deprivation headaches or eat too much in one sitting.

THE PROBLEM: SNACKING ON JUNK FOOD AND SUGAR

Do you rely on "comfort food" to keep you going in times of stress? This type of pleasure is short-lived. By indulging your sweet or fatty food tooth, you're actually stressing out your body and brain even further.

Fried foods can actually lower your immune system, affecting your body's ability to fight off colds and other illnesses. And sugar snacks might give you an immediate "high" or burst of energy, but you'll crash from that high as soon as your body digests the sugar, leaving you feeling cranky and out of it.

The Remedy: If at all possible, avoid fast foods altogether and replace processed sugary snacks with foods that are easy to digest and don't cause erratic spikes in your blood sugar. See page 206 for a list of healthy snack alternatives.

THE PROBLEM: CAFFEINE

It's no secret that caffeine—in coffee, many sodas, chocolate, and some teas (black tea, green tea)—can help you stay awake, and even make you more alert after drinking it. That's because your body releases adrenaline when caffeine hits your system. Yes, that would be the *same* adrenaline your body releases when you're experiencing stress. Though caffeine might give you a temporary boost, it also enhances the stress symptoms your body is experiencing. Plainly put, caffeine literally makes you more stressed out.

The Remedy: Skip the double latte and put a limit on your daily caffeine intake. If you have to drink caffeine, drink it in lower-caffeine sources like sodas or tea, and cut yourself off by early afternoon so you're not left wide-eyed and staring at the cracks in your ceiling at two a.m.

Practicing Good Nutrition

Now that you know what *not* to do, here's what you *can* do to ensure that what you eat and drink has a positive effect on the way your body responds to stress.

Create nutritional balance. The key to balance in your diet? *Don't go extreme.* No-carb, no-fat, or all-protein diets deprive your body of important nutrients. Your body needs a balance of carbs, fats, and protein to run efficiently, so eat it all (in moderation, of course).

Drink plenty of water. About 60 percent of your body is made up of water, so it should come as no surprise that H_2O is absolutely essential to your nutritional well-being. Water helps your body digest food, keeps your skin healthy, flushes your system of toxins, and keeps your brain sharp and alert. And you don't have to drink pure water to appreciate the benefits—natural fruit juices, teas (choose decaffeinated ones), and fluid replacement drinks like Gatorade, as well as fruits like cantaloupe, oranges, and watermelon, are all good sources of water.

Eat breakfast. You know the rumors about breakfast being the most important meal of the day? Well, they're true. It doesn't matter if you're running late or you think you're too busy to grab a bite first thing—skipping out on breakfast puts you at a disadvantage right off the bat when it comes to handling your daily stress. According to the American Dietetic Association, adolescents who regularly eat breakfast are in better shape to learn. "Breakfast eaters have higher school attendance, less tardiness, and fewer hunger-induced stomachaches in the morning. They concentrate better, solve problems more easily, and have better muscle coordination." There . . . 'nuff said.

Need a quick breakfast to get you through a busy day? Try drinking water or natural fruit juice with:

- Whole-wheat toast with peanut butter

- Low-fat yogurt with fresh fruit

- Whole-grain waffles

- Low-fat granola with skim, soy, or rice milk and sliced bananas

- Fruit and yogurt smoothie

Stock up on healthy, non-stress snacks. You can still practice good nutrition and snack at the same time—it's all about the choices you make. Here are some ideas for healthy snacks that may actually reduce stress symptoms:

- Popcorn (lightly buttered and salted)

- Apple with peanut butter

- Raw carrots or celery

- Nuts or trail mix
- Fruit (apples, bananas, grapes, strawberries, and other berries)
- Baked chips with guacamole
- Yogurt
- Hard-boiled egg
- Hummus and pita
- Quesadilla with sliced avocados and cheese
- Peanut butter and banana sandwich
- Fruit bar or energy bar
- Green Smoothie

Eat some afternoon carbohydrates. If you're a carb craver, you'll be pleased to know that research shows a midafternoon snack of simple carbohydrates can actually relieve your stress symptoms. According to scientist Dr. Judith Wurtman, carbohydrates like pretzels or popcorn cause your body to release a natural stress-relieving chemical called serotonin. This carb-created stress release only works in the afternoon, though, when your body's serotonin levels are naturally at their lowest point.

Don't forget the fiber. Since stress can cause your body to become constipated, eating a diet high in fiber can nip this problem in the bud by keeping things flowing. Great sources of fiber include oatmeal, whole-grain foods (bran cereal, multigrain bread), fresh fruits (especially apples and pears), dried fruits (like raisins or apricots), and fresh vegetables (root vegetables and raw vegetables).

208   Making It Stick

CHILL

Old (and unhealthy) eating habits can be hard to break. But don't worry—even if you're in a rut of eating fast food or making poor nutritional choices, all it takes is committing to your nutrition plan *now* to start experiencing the positive effects. Here are some foolproof ways to stay motivated:

- **Ask your family to join you** in stocking the house with healthy snacks and keeping unhealthy foods out of the pantry. If it's not there, you can't eat it. Why not just get rid of the temptations once and for all?

- **Keep a healthy snack in your backpack at all times.** A package of trail mix or an energy bar is perfect for a quick pick-me-up if you're starting to feel fatigue from hunger. Remember to replenish your snack stock so you'll have food on hand the next time you need it.

- **Get a reusable water bottle, and keep it filled and with you at all times.** Set a goal of drinking at least three water bottles each day.

- **Take a multivitamin.** Multivitamins can ensure that you get all the nutrients and vitamins you need in your diet, something that's especially important when your immune system is compromised because of stress. (Note that taking a multivitamin isn't a *substitute* for eating vitamin-rich food.)

- **Don't give in to stress-related food cravings right away.** Wait ten minutes between the craving of unhealthy food and actually eating something (sip some water while you wait), since within that time period you may choose not to eat anything at all, or you may opt to eat something healthier.

JOURNAL IT:

- **Keep a food journal for one
  week.** Keep track of everything you
  eat, and explore why you ate it and
  how it made you feel—emotionally,
  mentally, and physically. You might be surprised to
  see the patterns that emerge in your diet.

- **Write a list of five unhealthy nutritional habits**
  you fall into when you're experiencing stress and
  brainstorm alternative behaviors you could replace
  these habits with. This way you'll have a nutritional
  plan in place the next time the stress hits the fan.

Quiz

Do you know the difference between nutritional myths and
realities?

1. True   False   I can make up for bad eating habits simply
                  by taking multivitamins.

2. True   False   A food labeled "fat free" is a healthy snack.

3. True   False   Drinking black tea in moderate amounts
                  can reduce your physiological symptoms of
                  stress.

4. True   False   Drinking calorie- and caffeine-free soda has
                  the same effect on your body as drinking
                  water.

5. True   False   Being stressed out can cause your body to
                  lose important nutrients.

CHILL

ANSWERS

1. FALSE. Taking more than the recommended dose of a multivitamin can actually be detrimental to your health. The best way to make sure you're getting what you need is to eat a diet made up of food from all the food groups.

2. FALSE. Just because a food is fat free doesn't mean it is low calorie or that it has actual nutritional value.

3. TRUE. A recent study by the University College London found that drinking black tea actually reduces the amount of the stress hormone cortisol in the body.

4. FALSE. Even a soda that's free of calories and caffeine has chemicals in it that can be harmful to the body, including phosphoric acid. Too much phosphoric acid can eventually weaken your bones.

5. TRUE. People who are chronically stressed and anxious typically have faster metabolisms, which results in their bodies losing important nutrients like vitamins B and C more quickly than others.

CREATE A NUTRITION AFFIRMATION

Put your affirmation somewhere visible (maybe on your refrigerator or pantry door) as a reminder to yourself. Here are a few ideas to get you started:

- *When I eat well, I am giving myself the gift of health and balance.*
- *I make healthy food choices, which brings balance to my life.*
- *I am a healthy person who knows the value of taking care of my nutritional needs.*

Dear Debbie,

It seems like whenever the pressure is on at school, my best friend picks a fight with me. Like this year during finals, she was really mad at me, and so I had to deal with that stress plus trying to get good grades on my exams. How can I handle stress like this?

Shelby, age 16

Dear Shelby,

It sounds like your friend has some pretty bad timing when it comes to picking fights. For starters, during periods of extreme stress like midterms and finals, it's really important to take care of yourself by making sure you're getting enough sleep and keeping your body balanced by practicing good nutrition. Make sure you're drinking enough water, avoid overloading on caffeine (especially because this might make you more irritable with your friend), and fuel yourself throughout the day with small, healthy meals. Secondly, there's nothing wrong with telling your friend straight up that you care about her and want to resolve the situation, but it will have to wait until finals are over. Don't put more fuel on the fire by getting annoyed with her about her timing, since it will only heat up the conflict. Your priority during this stressful time should be to stay as balanced as possible, and this includes taking a break from friendship drama. Once your finals have passed, you can approach your friend again and try to work things out.

XOXO Debbie

DEBBIE'S SUPER FRUIT SMOOTHIE RECIPE

½ cup fat-free vanilla yogurt

½ cup frozen fruit (strawberries, mango, raspberries . . . whatever you fancy)

½ fresh banana

1 cup orange juice

3 ice cubes

Put all ingredients into blender (or into a large cup for immersion blender), and blend on high until completely smooth.

DEBBIE'S FAVORITE GREEN SMOOTHIE

1 cup water

1 cup raw spinach

½ cup raw kale

¼ cup vanilla yogurt

½ banana

1 cup of frozen berries

1 teaspoon honey

Put all ingredients into blender and blend on high until completely smooth.

EPILOGUE

So . . . how do you feel? At peace? More balanced? More *chill*? I hope so. And I hope that in reading this book you've identified a few stress-reducing strategies that suit your personality and lifestyle. If you can figure out what works best for you in managing your stress, you've already won half the battle.

Immediately after reading this book, you may experience a serious, positive shift in your balance and peace levels as you try out some of the tips included within. That's great! But be aware that as life goes on, stressful circumstances are bound to crop up that will put you to the test. When that happens, pick up *Chill* again, and flip through the sections that really speak to you for a quick stress-relief boost.

As I wrote at the beginning of this book, you don't have to be stressed if you don't want to. It's within your power and control to make the choice to say no to stress. In doing so, you're shouting a big, resounding yes to having a more balanced, healthy, and fulfilling life. Hey . . . you're worth it!